ADVANCE PRA

"Do not miss this rare opportunity to slide behind the glossy book jacket and sneak a peek between the pages, where one of Canada's foremost masters of mystery shares her secrets. Gail Bowen has been at the top of the mystery writing game for decades. With seeming effortlessness she blurs the boundary between writing a crackling good whodunit and elegant storytelling. Bowen's characters jump off the page with a realism that makes it seem as if they are the cast of a biography rather than works of fiction. Bowen knows how to build suspense with the same electrical intensity as a prairie howler building force on a dark, menacing horizon. How does she do it? Find out within the pages of *Sleuth*, a book with something for everyone, from newbie writer to practiced professional, from established mystery fan to beginning reader. With great insight, humour, unparalleled experience and interspersed with insights from Philo of Alexandra to Stephen King, Bowen delivers a master class. No one makes murder look so easy." ANTHONY BIDULKA, WINNER OF THE LAMBDA LITERARY AWARD FOR BEST MEN'S MYSTERY

"Books on how to write fiction tend toward two extremes: either they present a formula that is about as much fun as filling out an insurance form, or they are so woo-woo vague as to be no use at all. But Gail Bowen's *Sleuth*—informative, personal, and encouraging—is an excellent hands-on guide for anyone who wants to write a whodunit. As usual, Bowen comes up with a thoroughly engaging narrator—only this time it's her charming (and entirely too modest) self." GILES BLUNT, AUTHOR OF THE JOHN CARDINAL MYSTERIES

"A masterful mix of accumulated wisdom and practical writing tips." BARBARA FRADKIN, TWO-TIME WINNER OF THE ARTHUR ELLIS AWARD FOR BEST NOVEL

"Elegant, informative and deeply humane, Gail Bowen's *Sleuth* is a wonderfully insightful guide into the art of not only crime-writing, but the art of fiction itself." AUSMA ZEHANAT KHAN, AUTHOR OF *The Unquiet Dead*

"In her primer *Sleuth*, Gail Bowen has taken the mystery out of writing mysteries, and in her insightful and humorous and compendious way (she cleverly cites Elmore Leonard, Richard Price and others) Gail actually describes the building blocks that form the basis of any novel, mystery or not. I expect this book will become a standard text for writing classes of all levels." IAN HAMILTON, AUTHOR OF THE AVA LEE NOVELS

"Psst! Want to write a wildly successful mystery novel? Buy and read Gail Bowen's *Sleuth*. You couldn't be in better hands." ALAN BRADLEY, *New York Times* BESTSELLING AUTHOR OF THE FLAVIA DE LUCE SERIES

GAIL BOWEN
ON WRITING MYSTERIES

University of Regina Press

Printed and bound in Canada at Marquis. The text of this book is printed on 100% post-consumer recycled paper with earth-friendly vegetable-based inks.

Cover and text design: Duncan Campbell, University of Regina Press
Copy editor: Dallas Harrison
Proofreader: Kristine Douaud
Cover art: Vintage engraving of a magnifying glass isolated on white
© Can Stock Photo / HypnoCreative

Library and Archives Canada Cataloguing in Publication

Bowen, Gail, 1942-, author
Sleuth : Gail Bowen on writing mysteries.

Includes bibliographical references.
Issued in print and electronic formats.
ISBN 978-0-88977-524-4 (softcover).– ISBN 978-0-88977-525-1 (PDF)
–ISBN 978-0-88977-526-8 (HTML)

1. Detective and mystery stories—Authorship.
I. Title. II. Title: Gail Bowen on writing mysteries.

PN3377.5.D4B69 2018 808.3'872 C2017-907457-1

10 9 8 7 6 5 4 3 2 1

U OF R PRESS

University of Regina Press, University of Regina
Regina, Saskatchewan, Canada, S4S 0A2
TEL: (306) 585-4758 FAX: (306) 585-4699
WEB: www.uofrpress.ca

We acknowledge the support of the Canada Council for the Arts for our publishing program. We acknowledge the financial support of the Government of Canada. / Nous reconnaissons l'appui financier du gouvernement du Canada. This publication was made possible with support from Creative Saskatchewan's Creative Industries Production Grant Program.

CONTENTS

WRITERS ON WRITING

The Writers on Writing book series offers readers witty, conversational reflections on a wide range of craft-related topics, as well as practical advice for writers and the writing life at any level. The books are accessible and handy, yet they don't shy away from the challenges of writing. They'll become your friends. Think sitting down in a coffee shop in conversation with a smart, friendly, veteran author. Part inspiration, part advice, part anecdote—total oxygen after all those stuffy writing textbooks.

Jeanette Lynes, Series Editor

FOR MORE INFORMATION ON THE
WRITERS ON WRITING SERIES, CONTACT:

University of Regina Press
3737 Wascana Parkway
Regina SK S4S 0A2
uofrpress@uregina.ca
www.uofrpress.ca

CHAPTER 1

THE PUSH TOWARD WRITING

I began writing when I was forty-three. I mention this because a surprising number of people believe that, if they haven't written something significant by the time they're forty, it's game over. Luckily for us all, the muscles required for writing are not the same as the muscles required for ballet. By the time you're forty, fifty, sixty, seventy, eighty, or ninety plus, the well is primed. You have something to offer that no one else does, so if you have always longed to write this is the time to get started because this is the time you have.

I became a writer by chance. My youngest son's godfather, Ron Marken, a professor of English at the University of Saskatchewan, was editing a book titled *An Easterner's Guide to Western Canada/A Westerner's Guide to Eastern Canada.* The book was what I always think of as "an airport book"—the kind of book you buy at the airport kiosk and read and leave on the plane. The premise was fun. Writers from western Canada were to write humorous accounts of how effete easterners could survive out here in the wild and woolly west, and writers from eastern Canada would respond with humorous accounts of how we bumpkin westerners could survive in the rarefied atmosphere of Toronto or Montreal.

That was a busy time in my life. My husband and I had three kids, two dogs, and an old house crumbling around our ears. I was an assistant professor of English at the university, and Ted was a speechwriter for the premier of our province. It was a typical frantic Sunday afternoon when Ron called and asked me for help. After describing the book, he said the person who had submitted the entry for Saskatchewan had written something poetic, elegiac, and utterly unsuitable for a book supposed to be amusing and a little bawdy. The writer refused to rewrite the piece, and Ron's deadline for getting the westerners' half of the book to the publisher was the following Wednesday. He asked me if I could write something.

My plate was already full, and I am by nature risk-averse, so I thanked Ron for thinking of me and said no. When I told my husband about my conversation with Ron, Ted reminded me that Ron was our son Nathaniel's godfather and that perhaps I should rethink my decision. I called Ron back and said I'd take a shot at writing the Saskatchewan entry.

In that moment, our whole lives changed. As Stephen King once wrote, "Life turns on a dime. Sometimes towards us, but more often it spins away, flirting and flaunting as it goes: 'so long honey, it was good while it lasted, wasn't it?'" That afternoon in the cheerful chaos of dogs, kids, and papers to grade, the dime spun toward me, and the good luck it brought with it has lasted a very long time.

My entry in the *Guide* was a letter written by a private-school girl from Toronto who has followed her beloved to begin married life in rural Saskatchewan. I was a private-school girl from Toronto who had followed my beloved to begin married life in rural Saskatchewan, so I was writing what I knew. It was a fun piece, and the publisher liked it enough to suggest that Ron and I write a series of letters between a private-school girl in Toronto and her beloved, one of the sodbusters who came to Saskatchewan to make his fortune.

Ron and I soon discovered that a young man busting sod twelve hours a day didn't have much to write about to his sweetheart, so we chose instead to write a book called *1919: The Love Letters of George and Adelaide*. *1919* is the story of three young people whose lives were altered forever by the Great War. George and his friend, Roger, are both Saskatchewan boys. George has been crippled and Roger blinded in battle. Adelaide is the volunteer nurse they meet at a convalescent hospital in Toronto. The novella traces their efforts to come to terms with their changed lives in a country that came of age in the years during and after the First World War.

1919 was well if quietly received, but here comes the good part. Years later Susan Ferley of the Globe Theatre in Regina asked us to adapt the book as a play, and the resulting production led to a chat at a table for ten with Prince Charles, who asked me about my Joanne Kilbourn series and said he regretted there were not yet audio versions of my books he could listen to while he drove. Clearly he had been briefed, but I still smile when I imagine Charles and Camilla whizzing through the countryside in their Land Rover listening to an audio version of *Deadly Appearances*.

Dancing in Poppies netted me another visit with a royal when a special production of the play was mounted for Charles's brother, Prince Edward, the royal patron of the Globe Theatre. After the performance, the actors, the director, and Ron and I had dinner with Prince Edward, who was funny, charming, and thoughtful—everything a prince should be. He told us his mom and dad liked nothing better than to sit the family down after Sunday dinner and listen to a recording of radio bloopers.

After writing *1919*, I was eager to continue writing. Ron wasn't, so the Joanne Kilbourn mystery series was born. *Deadly Appearances*, the first book in the series, was published in 1990. *The Winners Circle*, the seventeenth Joanne Kilbourn novel, was published in 2017.

Deadly Appearances got nice reviews, racked up modest sales, and then—serendipity—was nominated for the W. H. Smith Best First Novel award. It didn't win, but in a competitive industry in which first novels can easily be buried the buzz from the nomination kept *Deadly Appearances* alive. And then—further serendipity—Peter Gzowski, host of *Morningside*, a national radio program that had a huge audience of book-loving, book-buying listeners, read *Deadly Appearances* and invited me to be interviewed on his show. Peter and I clicked. He once gave me five extra minutes of interview time because I was the only person who had ever used the word *lugubrious* on *Morningside*. I made many return visits to the show, and over the years I continued close relationships with Peter, my great friend Shelagh Rogers (also a lover of mystery books), and the CBC.

My first three books were published by Douglas and McIntyre, a fine but at that time smallish Vancouver publishing house. I'd just finished my fourth novel, *A Colder Kind of Death*, when Douglas and McIntyre decided to go out of mysteries, but the publisher, Rob Sanders, recommended my series to McClelland and Stewart, a much larger publisher with a much larger budget for publicity and distribution. *A Colder Kind of Death* won the Arthur Ellis award for Best Crime Novel of the year, and I continued on my strange and serendipitous journey, churning out one book every two years and selling enough books to keep being published.

The first six books in the Joanne Kilbourn series became made-for-TV movies starring Wendy Crewson and Victor Garber. Someone once told me the chances of having a book that has been optioned for a film actually reach the screen are about the same as the chances of being hit by lightning. So I've been hit by lightning six times.

Here's how it happened. My agent, Bella Pomer, was also novelist Carol Shields's agent. A production company just starting up called Shaftesbury Films made a movie from one of Carol's books. Bella ran into Christina Jennings, the CEO of Shaftesbury, at the premiere of Carol's movie and mentioned my series. Christina asked Bella to send her a fax with information about my books.

I'm certain all movie companies get hundreds of proposals; I'm equally certain most of those proposals go straight into the shredder, but Shaftesbury Films shared an office with another small company, Deirdre Bowen Casting. Fortuitously, Deirdre was at the fax machine when Bella's proposal came in. Intrigued by the cover page's reference to "The Bowen Books," Deirdre went to the bookstore around the corner and bought a copy of *Deadly Appearances*. She read it, liked it, and told Christina Jennings about it, and I was on my way.

The Joanne Kilbourn movies have been shown all over the world, and they're still popping up on Canadian and American channels with regularity. The production values are first-rate; the actors, especially Crewson and Garber, are excellent; and the movies themselves are entertaining. People, including me, really enjoy them. If you sense a certain reticence in my endorsement, you're perceptive. As enjoyable as the movies are, they don't bear much resemblance to my books.

After Louis Begley, the author of *About Schmidt*, attended the premiere of the 2002 movie starring Jack Nicholson, he was dumbfounded. When Begley told the film's director he was surprised that everything about his book had been changed for the movie, the director smiled and said, "Look on the bright side. All we used was the title. You can sell the rest to another movie studio." Later Begley, genuinely pleased by the movie, said in an interview the experience taught him that the relationship between a writer's book and the movie made from it is the same as the relationship between an ox and an Oxo cube.

After I saw the Kilbourn movies, I understood what Begley meant. The movies, all set in Saskatchewan, were filmed in Toronto. Shaftesbury Films made a heroic effort to film the movies in Saskatchewan, but it was simply cheaper to make them in Toronto, so there are no shots of brilliant prairie sunsets or abandoned grain elevators. Because our province has a strong eastern European heritage, many of my characters have Ukrainian surnames. In *Deadly Appearances*, the retired premier's surname is Dowhanuik, and the name of the candidate Joanne Kilbourn supports to replace him is Andy Boychuk. The movies anglicized all the names.

Christina Jennings was extraordinarily sensitive to me as a writer facing the exigencies of a world about which I knew nothing. She sent me scripts, listened to my concerns, and if possible dealt with what, in my mind, were genuine problems. For example, the opening scene of an early script for *Murder at the Mendel* (later *Love and Murder*) had fifteen-year-old Joanne masturbating. I have no problem with anybody masturbating, but that particular self-pleasuring had no connection with the story we wanted to tell. I pointed that out to Christina, and in the revised script Joanne kept her hands on top of the covers, and her actions remained focused on the plot.

Having children and grandchildren and living in Regina, a city where the fact that I'm a writer is regarded as pleasant but not earthshaking, have kept my ego in check. That said, I admit that, the first time I walked onto the movie set of one of my books, I felt a thrill. More than anything, my feelings might simply have reflected my background. I grew up knowing how important it is for people to have jobs that honour their skills and pay them decent salaries for their work. I'm not ashamed to say that seeing over 100 people on set whose work was being honoured and who were earning decent salaries because of a book I had written brought a lump to my throat.

One hot day on an interminably long streetcar ride in downtown Toronto, that lucky dime that spun toward me when I said yes to writing the piece for *An Easterner's Guide to Western Canada* spun toward me again.

Most of my career as an English professor was spent at First Nations University of Canada in Regina. It was a great job, and I loved my work, but I soon became aware of the struggle many students–Indigenous and non-Indigenous–have with literacy. It is impossible to overstate the importance of being able to read and write competently and confidently, yet many adults in Canada are unable to do either. The inability to read closes many doors–professionally and personally–but perhaps most seriously it erodes a person's sense of worth.

In the back of my mind, I always thought that when I retired I'd like to write a book for adults struggling with literacy. What I envisioned was a book with a strong plot, interesting characters, a protagonist with whom a reader could identify, written using words and sentence structures that would make the book accessible to the emerging reader. We all have great plans for retirement, and my plan to write a book for reluctant readers probably would have gone the way of many of my good intentions, but once again fate introduced a happy confluence.

Back to that streetcar ride. I was thumbing my BlackBerry when I noticed a message from Orca Books in Victoria. I knew Orca as an excellent publisher of children's books, and I assumed this was just some announcement, but I was bored, so I opened the message. The email was from Bob Tyrrell, at the time the owner and publisher of Orca Books, asking me if I'd be interested in participating in a new series for–you guessed it–adults struggling with literacy. As soon as I got home, I called Bob.

I've written four Rapid Reads books. They are mysteries and feature a very cool guy named Charlie Dowhanuik, about whom you'll hear more later. The books are read by people in literacy groups, by high school kids struggling with their studies, by men and women in prisons, and by people who just want a quick read. I've visited many of these groups, including those in prison, and I'm both proud and grateful when I see the Charlie D series in their libraries.

Canadian writer Robertson Davies has a line I'm fond of: "When life pushes you in a certain direction, it's spiritual suicide to resist." I'm very thankful life pushed me toward writing, and I'm glad my husband was there to make certain I followed through.

Now it's time to go back to the beginning.

CHAPTER 2

GETTING STARTED

In my first year at the University of Toronto, I won a thirty dollar book prize for having the highest grade in Introductory English (Beowulf to Pope). My professor noted that I wrote with conviction, flair, and passion. I was a rising star, no doubt about it, but there was a small and seemingly insignificant cloud on my horizon. In the otherwise laudatory note that accompanied my prize, the professor noted there was "a certain fluffiness" in my writing I "might wish to address." I had no idea what he was talking about, nor did I care to know.

I had won a prize, and when I went back to university in the fall I would be a "sophomore," a term that my English professor told us on the last day of classes was a portmanteau of the Greek words *sophos* meaning "wise" and *moros* meaning "foolish." I ignored him. I was not "a wise fool." I had won a prize.

The following September, when I walked into Dr. Ellen Woolf's class on The Changing Face of Women in the British Novel, I didn't realize my life was about to change. The air was crisp with the promise of autumn, and Toronto was brilliant with the vivid hues of the September palette. In the early 1960s, Woolf, a PhD who was both young and female, was an anomaly at Victoria College. Like all professors at the college in those days, Dr. Woolf taught wearing a simple black academic robe. Her voice shook when she introduced herself, but her nervousness fell away as she turned her back to the class, picked up the chalk, and wrote "The Elements of the Novel" on the blackboard in a strong, clear hand. Without speaking, she wrote a list beneath the title.

1. Theme
2. Protagonist, Secondary Characters, and Minor Characters
3. Narrative Perspective
4. Setting
5. Plot and Structure
6. Style and Syntax

Still with her back to the class, she said, "These are a novelist's tools. The choices the novelist makes about how she will use each of these tools will determine whether the writer succeeds in reaching her goals."

For the next fifty minutes, my pen never left the page. I walked out of Dr. Woolf's class chagrined at how little I knew but determined to learn more. Dr. Woolf had explained in clear and accessible language how, by analyzing the ways in which a writer uses each of the elements of fiction, the reader can recognize why a novel succeeds or why, as a professor of mine in graduate school would later say, a novel "goes off the rails."

Like Saul on the road to Damascus, the scales fell from my eyes. Suddenly I understood why, in characterizing my long-on-style/short-on-substance writing as "fluffy," my first-year professor had been right on the money. A piece of writing, regardless of the genre, must have good "bones." When the shimmering prose fades, the reader must be left with something solid that enlarges his or her mind. The hundreds of pieces of writing I would later complete have a sobering variety of flaws, but none of them is fluffy.

From the day I stepped into Dr. Woolf's classroom, I have asked myself two simple questions before I begin to write: "What do I hope to achieve with this piece of writing?" and "How can I best use the tools at hand to achieve my goal?"

During the early years of my university teaching, my writing was pretty much limited to academic papers. In 1990, twenty-nine years after I completed Dr. Woolf's class, I wrote *Deadly Appearances*, the first of the Joanne Kilbourn mystery novels. In 2017, *The Winners Circle*, the seventeenth novel in the series, was published. Dr. Woolf's lessons about how a novel works have informed every page I have written, and you will see her fingerprints throughout *Sleuth*.

You will also see evidence of what I absorbed, seemingly by osmosis, during the summers I spent in passionate, indiscriminate, blissful reading of mysteries, starting with Aesop. Remember the tale of the fox that, unlike all the other animals in the lion's kingdom, refuses the invitation to visit the lion in his cave because the fox, an early master of ratiocination, noted that, though there were many footprints going into the cave of the king of the jungle, there was none coming out?

From Aesop, I moved on to Sir Arthur Conan Doyle (much later, when I was the writer-in-residence at the Toronto Reference Library, I spent a fascinating three months in an exact replica of Conan Doyle's office, complete with first editions, a deerstalker hat, samples of the three kinds of pipe Sherlock Holmes smoked—a briar, a black clay, and a cherry wood—and very briefly a hypodermic needle). In my graduating year, I split my holiday reading: July was for the golden age of mystery (Dorothy L. Sayers, Marjorie Allingham, Josephine Tey, and Agatha Christie); August was for the hard-boiled dicks (Dashiell Hammett, Raymond Chandler, Robert Parker, et al.). Somewhere along the line, I lost my heart to Nero Wolfe and Archie Goodwin, love affairs that endure to this day.

The insights I gleaned from the hours I spent reading mysteries when I escaped to Queen's Park from my soul-crushingly tedious summer job, or on the raft at Cameron Lake slathered with baby oil, have also informed my work. Anecdotes, tips, and examples of what I learned on those steamy summer days about how to write a mystery will pop up regularly throughout this book.

When I teach creative writing, I'm cautious about the advice I offer. It's tempting and all too easy for an instructor to guide a student into writing the book the instructor herself would write, so I try not to be heavy-handed with the red pen.

That said, I have no hesitation in telling you that, as a passionate mystery reader, you already know a great deal about how to write a mystery. Through your wide reading, you have zeroed in on the kinds of mysteries that bring you the greatest sense of fulfillment. Man Booker Prize winner Hilary Mantel offers some solid advice:

"Write a book you'd like to read. If you wouldn't read it, why would anybody else?" Your goal as a writer is to create the kind of novel that most pleases you as a reader.

Before I began to write *Deadly Appearances*, I made notes on the mystery novels I had found most satisfying. I discovered that, though I had enjoyed many brilliant stand-alone mysteries, I was powerfully drawn to mystery *series*, and those series shared certain characteristics.

Robust plotting is generally accepted to be the backbone of the mystery, but when I looked at my list I recognized how often I was drawn to novels by elements often regarded as ancillary to plot: books with protagonists who were human and humane and left me wanting to be in their company again, and a repertory company of engaging secondary characters who, when they appeared, always sparked my interest. My bedside table was always piled with books that drew me into a world that reflected the world I knew: a place of diversity in ethnicity, sexual orientation, religious and political beliefs, and educational background. Finally, I saw again and again that I was drawn to books that explored the social and political issues that confront us all.

With Dr. Woolf's list of "The Elements of the Novel" beside me, I jotted down possibilities (written in pencil, not in stone) about themes, potential protagonists and secondary characters, the advantages and disadvantages of various narrative perspectives, and settings that would allow me to say what I wanted to say. I left decisions about plot, structure, style, and syntax for another day, but when I looked at what I *had* written I began to get ideas on plot and structure. The seeds of my first Joanne Kilbourn novel had been planted, and they were already sprouting. I was on my way.

Your decisions about how to use the elements of fiction to write your book will differ from mine. There are no one-size-fits-all answers for mystery writers, but Dr. Woolf's list will guide you to decisions that are the best for you. The mystery genre is amazingly accommodating. Walk into any mystery bookstore, and you'll discover a book to satisfy the interests of any reader. There are thrillers, police procedurals, and cozies with cats and recipes. There are mysteries for people with a taste for the high life or the low life, for quilting, for blood and gore, for forensics, for gardening, or for horse racing. There are mysteries with protagonists who have taken holy orders, and mysteries whose heroes seem to have working relationships with Lucifer. Sleuths can be young, old, or in between; gay, straight, lesbian, questioning, or transgender; or of any ethnicity or religion. They can even write mysteries and live in a picturesque village like Cabot Cove, Maine. Someone has to write books for all these readers. And that someone can be you.

There are many reasons why writers choose to work in the mystery genre. Here are five.

First, the narrator of Evelyn Waugh's short story "Work Suspended" offers a modest explanation:

> There seemed few ways of which a writer need not be ashamed by which he could make a decent living. To produce something, saleable in large quantities to the public, which had absolutely nothing of myself in it; to sell something for which the kind of people I liked and respected would have a use; that was what I sought, and detective stories fulfilled the purpose.

Second, the endurance of Sir Arthur Conan Doyle's Sherlock Holmes is eloquent testimony of the "use" of detective stories. Sherlock first appeared in 1887, and here we are 130 years later with movies and at least two television series—the DVDs of which, interestingly, are sold with copies of Conan Doyle's books. Sherlock's deadly battle with Professor James Moriarty at Reichenbach Falls is a classic example of the eternal struggle between good and evil, law and lawlessness, at the heart of every mystery. That never-ending struggle plays a pivotal role in understanding the mystery's continuing appeal. The philosopher John Gray has a provocative explanation of the lasting appeal of Sherlock Holmes: "When the future seems more than usually uncertain and the present is troubling, it's natural to look to the past."

Third, Ian Rankin, author of the twenty-book-long-and-going-strong Inspector John Rebus series, points to another factor that draws readers to the mystery genre: "Readers realize that along with compelling narrative, crime fiction says important things about the state of the modern world and asks tough questions, making us think about our societies, our institutions and ourselves."

Fourth, American critic Terry Teachout, a passionate fan of Rex Stout's Nero Wolfe series, praises it "as tasteful, impeccably crafted pieces of writing whose sole purpose is to amuse." Teachout says of the series that "They've been giving me pleasure for forty years, and I expect them to do so for many years to come." In my opinion, giving readers pleasure is reason enough for a writer to choose to work in the mystery genre.

Fifth, in his *New York Times* review of Richard Price's *The Whites* Michael Connelly (a fine crime writer himself) points to a timely and compelling reason why writers choose crime fiction. Connelly quotes Price's response to an interviewer who asked why Price devoted so much of his considerable literary talent to crime fiction and film scripts featuring criminals. Price said that when you circle around a murder long enough you get to know a city. Connelly believes that this answer "crystallized what many writers knew and attempted to practice. That is, he considered the crime novel something more than a puzzle and an entertainment; he saw it as societal reflection, documentation and investigation."

Five solid reasons to get started. And one final, gentle push: as Vladimir Nabokov notes in "The Art of Literature and Commonsense," "The pages are still blank, but there is a miraculous feeling of the words all being there, written in invisible ink and clamoring to become visible."

CHAPTER 3

PREWRITING YOUR MYSTERY

WRITING IN THE CRACKS

There is an axiom that's been around since people began putting quills into inkpots: *writers write, and when they are not writing they are thinking about writing.*

Many years ago I received a book titled *The Psychiatrist's Wife's Guide to Housekeeping* as a wedding gift. The book's title did not reach out to me, but the psychiatrist's wife offered a piece of advice that has made it possible for me (wife of one, mother of three, grandmother of seven, dog owner, and until recently full-time academic) to sustain a career as a writer. The unnamed wife of the unnamed psychiatrist said that, when she saw a spot on her kitchen cupboard, she did not say, "As soon as I have a significant block of time, I will clean my kitchen"; instead, she picked up a damp cloth, wiped off the spot, and got on with her life.

When I began writing fiction, I knew I would never have a significant block of time in which to write. I would have to do the most I could with the time I had. Writing in the cracks has become second nature to me, but remembering an encounter I had with a workshop participant a few years ago in Banff has prodded me to include a section here on how to manage that rarest of all commodities: writing time.

Let me take you back. It was a five-star day, as all days in Banff are—cerulean skies, snow-capped mountains, and sunshine so warm that, though it was early May, the bravest among us were wearing shorts. The emerging mystery writers had gone through the ritual sniffing of the instructor (me) and their workshop colleagues and pronounced us satisfactory. We were all looking forward to a terrific week, so I was surprised when Ms. X, one of our group members, took me aside after lunch and told me she was depressed.

I was incredulous. Ms. X was an intelligent and charming woman who, for the next five days, would be holed up with her laptop in a room with a million-dollar view. We were surrounded by hiking trails of heart-stopping beauty. Her work would be studied and clucked over by congenial peers and a moderately successful professional writer; most importantly, three times a day, she could eat fabulous meals prepared by someone else. In short, she was in writer's paradise.

That, as it turned out, was the rub. As Ms. X and I talked, it became clear that the prospect of "Paradise Lost" was causing her angst. The loss she feared was not that of the mountains, the instructor, the peers, or even the superlative food. What she dreaded most was that, at the end of the week, she would, in her words, have to put her writing "aside" until she was able to come up with "another significant block of time." Her statement stopped me in my tracks, but my discussion with her that day produced some points worth considering here.

Unless you are lucky enough to be a trust-fund baby, you are dealing with a real life that contains a number of people in hot competition for slices of your day. It's unwise to ignore the demands of children, life partners, and employers, so as a writer with a real life you must learn to make the most of every free moment.

The craft of writing involves three distinct processes—prewriting, writing, and editing—and they are equally important. I estimate that, before I retired from full-time teaching, I spent less than one-tenth of my writing time with my laptop. Now I've probably upped the ratio to one-third. Of the other two-thirds, one-third is dedicated to editing, and one-third takes place when I'm walking with my husband, peeling spuds, playing with our grandkids and our dog, taking a shower, reading old *New Yorkers*, or staring at the wall. These activities do not take time away from my writing; on the contrary, they nourish and sustain it. Every hour spent in prewriting rewards me richly when I sit down at my desk and begin to write. It will be the same for you.

Creativity is elusive. The closest I can come to explaining it is through Stephen King's mischievous metaphor of "the boys in the basement." King says that, as he goes about the ordinary business of living, the boys in the basement are hard at work developing plot lines, filling out characters, coming up with snatches of dialogue. When King sits down in front of his computer, the boys in the basement send up their gifts.

This metaphor is seductive, and obviously it works for King, but most of us have to accept the fact that, when it comes to the heavy lifting, the writer has to do his or her share. As resourceful as the boys in the basement are, they must be fed, and the only person who can feed them is the writer. Seemingly the hunger of these boys is insatiable, but there are strategies for filling these bottomless pits.

One is to keep your well of ideas full. In *Flaubert's Parrot*, Julian Barnes's protagonist notes that "The best life for a writer is the life which helps him write the best books he can." Deciding on the "best life" for you as a writer is an individual decision. Barnes quotes Flaubert: "The writer must wade into life as into the sea, but only up to the navel. . . . It isn't the drunkard who writes the drinking song; on the other hand, it isn't the teetotaler either." No one will ever confuse my writing with that of Gustave Flaubert, but like him, when it comes to combining the solitary act of writing with the far-from-solitary business of living a full and varied life, I need both.

Do whatever you need to do to get your juices flowing. Take the time to look around you. Keep your antennae quivering at all times. Buy a notebook–the paper kind–with pockets in which you can tuck in whatever strikes your fancy: found poems, clippings from newspapers and magazines, pieces of your own work you need to edit.

Poet Ted Hughes speaks of the importance of "recording moments, fleeting impressions, overheard dialogue, your own sorrows, bewilderments and joys." Heed his words. As journalist Bill D. Moyers says, "Creativity is piercing the mundane to find the marvelous." Take note of encounters with people who fire your imagination.

For me, a single sentence in a TV interview with a famously shrewd CEO was so powerfully revealing that it inspired a character. When a reporter asked the CEO about the employees who would be laid off by his restructuring of the company of which he was assuming control, he said "There are always casualties" and moved smartly along to his next point. Those four words took me into the mind of someone whose outlook could not have been more different from my own. At first, I was simply gobsmacked by the executive's ruthlessness, his indifference to the lives of the men and women who would be displaced, but then I stepped back and tried to see the situation from his perspective. The company he was restructuring had been skimming the trees for months, and it was about to crash and burn. The CEO saw what needed to be done, did it, and saved the company and the jobs of over 100 people. That CEO became the model for Leland Hunter, a significant character in my novel *Kaleidoscope*. Leland is a multimillionaire developer whose motto is "Never ask permission; if it becomes necessary, ask forgiveness." His principles are antithetical to everything my protagonist believes, but in creating Leland I was governed by the gentle words of Philo of Alexandria (25 B.C.E.–50 C.E.): "Be kind, for everyone you meet is carrying a great burden." It was tempting for me to make Leland a villain, but remembering Philo's sage advice I looked kindly at the CEO on whom Leland was modelled, and when I understood more about the burdens that CEO carried I was able to make Leland a character about whom Joanne (and the reader) could care.

Insights into the mind and heart of "the other" are always worth recording in your notebook. These revelations will help you to develop "layered" secondary characters who will add breadth and depth to your novel, and sometimes these insights will lead you to create a character strong enough to play a significant role in your work.

The character of Charlie Dowhanuik, a hip, brilliant, angry young man with a birthmark that covers half his face, had its genesis in a two-minute encounter I had on a train to Vancouver. A stunningly beautiful young woman and her boyfriend boarded the train at Jasper, Alberta. Both were dressed for hiking. The young man had a large port-wine birthmark that covered his right cheek like a blood mask. He was wearing a T-shirt, and like too many of us I didn't know where to look, so I lowered my eyes and read the message on his shirt. "Beauty is in the eye of the be-holder." He saw that I'd noticed the words and smiled. "Do you want to check out the back of my shirt?" He pivoted, and I saw that the back showed the logo of a popular brand of beer. I was puzzled until he turned again to face me, and I realized I'd misread the message on his shirt. The sentence was "Beauty is in the eye of the beer-holder." "Love it," I said. We both laughed, and the young man and his girlfriend went to their compartment.

I never saw him again. However, the memory of that young man and of the grace with which he carried his burden stayed with me, and Charlie Dowhanuik, the angry, funny, deeply empathetic host of a late-night radio call-in show was born. Charlie is a recurring character in the Joanne Kilbourn series, and, when I was asked to write a mystery novella for Orca's high-interest/ low-vocabulary series of Rapid Reads, I chose Charlie as my protagonist. Readers liked *Love You to Death*, so I wrote three more Rapid Reads for the Charlie D series and two Charlie D mystery plays for the CBC.

A small but vivid fictional world grew from one brief train encounter.

Taking note of the telling details that reveal the minds and hearts of our fellow and sister human beings will provide you with tasty and nourishing chunks of this and that to throw into the stew that the boys in the basement wolf down with such gusto. And the boys will reward you. When–finally–you get a chance to open your laptop, you will have all sorts of material to help you fill that blank screen. As P. D. James said, "Open your mind to new experiences, particularly to the study of other people. Nothing that happens to a writer–however happy, however tragic–is ever wasted."

One of the many virtues of prewriting, of course, is that you can do it anywhere. A friend of mine schooled by the Ursulines remembers the Mother Superior impressing on her girls the truth that no opportunity should be wasted. "When you're on a bus, pray for the conversion of the people on the bus," the good sister would say. These are useful words to remember. As a mystery writer, you're spared the imperative to save the souls of your fellow passengers, but you can take note of their physical appearance and your speculation about their inner lives. Why is that mountain of a man with the tattoos and the ponytail immersed in a knitting book? Does the bass fiddle case that scowling girl is struggling with really contain a bass fiddle or something more sinister? Is anybody on the bus looking at *you* through narrowed eyes?

I have found inspiration in a pleasant, matronly woman dusting off plastic fetuses as she set up a pro-life booth at the university; in a politician taking a drink of water from a thermos at a political picnic (in fact, my first novel, *Deadly Appearances*, is set in motion by that single act); in a woman in my gynecologist's office who told me she was dealing with her ex-husband's defection by visiting every city and town she and her once beloved had lived in together so she could work out exactly when the fault line in their marriage had deepened into a crevice.

Without breaking into a sweat, I could give you 100 similar examples, but I hope my point is clear. None of these potentially fruitful moments came from a time when I was closeted away in my office. All came from times when I was fully engaged in the ordinary tasks and rhythms of living.

I once told a Grade 8 class that one of the things I liked best about being a writer was the fact that it made me a good live-er. They thought I was hilarious, but it is the truth. Good writers are good live-ers. They live life to the fullest: eyes bright, ears flapping, nose twitching, antennae on full alert. As screenwriter and novelist Nora Ephron famously remarked, "Writers are cannibals. Everything is copy." Everything that comes into the writer's world is potential material, so keep your world large, and take notes.

RESEARCHING YOUR NOVEL

> *Research, factual accuracy, lays the base for plausible fiction, for it actually enables suspension of disbelief in readers by building their trust.*–Helen Benedict

Research plays a key role in all three parts of the writing process: prewriting, writing, and editing. For the crime writer, the prewriting phase is a continuous act of discovery—of acquiring accurate knowledge of police work, forensics, law, and scores of other things about which most of us know very little. And accuracy matters.

There's an old saying that a fly in the soup doesn't spoil the soup, but it does spoil the experience. Don't spoil your reader's experience. Don't stint on the research. I learned this lesson the hard way.

Only 1 of 3,000 tortoiseshell cats is male. In an early novel in the Joanne Kilbourn series, Joanne finds a feral cat and takes it to a vet to have it checked out before it becomes part of her family. After a thorough examination, including a peek at the cat's genitals, the vet declares that the tortoiseshell cat Joanne found is a male. Her daughter names the cat Benny. A happy ending—that is, until the book was published and the letters chiding me for my mistake started to roll in. Alert cat lovers pointed out (1) that tortoiseshell cats are almost always female and (2) that even the biggest dolt who ever wandered into the School of Veterinary Medicine would be able to lift a kitten's tail. The opening just under the tail is the anus. Below the anus is the genital opening, a round hole in males and a vertical slit in females. So now I know, and so do you.

By training, I'm an academic. I once picked up a mystery in which members of an English department were being bumped off because a colleague was desperate to become chair of the department. Anyone who has ever sat through a university departmental meeting knows that *no one* has ever been driven to murder by the desire to become a department chair. Most of us (including me) grimly take our turn as chair and leave the office saying "never again." I did not buy that book.

I have heard more than one writer excuse sloppy research by saying that, because they are writing fiction, it doesn't matter if they just "make stuff up." Lawyers know that isn't true. A maxim from Roman law is as true for crime fiction writers as it is in the courtroom. *Falsus in uno, falsus in omnibus*—"False in one thing, false in everything." For lawyers, this principle means that a witness who is false in one matter will be false in other matters. For readers, it means that a writer who gets something verifiable wrong can't be trusted when she creates the events of her story. The need to "get it right" will lead you into unfamiliar territory. The insights you gain from your journeys will make you a stronger writer and a more complete human being.

The experts I've consulted are immensely generous about answering questions and offering information. I welcome the facts, but even more I welcome the glimpses into their world their answers give me. A young doctor of my acquaintance told me that, when a large number of ambulances arrive at the ER carrying critically injured accident victims, the medical team makes quick judgments about which of the injured are "salvageable"—the cool pragmatism of that word gave me more insight into that young doctor's world than a dozen journal articles ever could.

In recent Joanne Kilbourn novels, a retired police officer has helped me to verify police procedure. His information about the protocol of police work is always detailed and accurate, but his informal comments about the inner lives of police officers are invaluable. Without him, I never would have known how the rush of emotion officers experience when they arrive at a crime scene often causes them to misread information and pursue leads that go nowhere. He also said that, as days of an investigation turn into weeks, a smouldering anger envelopes every officer on the case.

The last time he and I were together, my friend told me about going into the morgue and watching as a pathologist performed an autopsy on a two-year-old who had choked. As the autopsy continued, another pathologist stroked the boy's leg gently and continued talking to the boy as if he were still alive, not just a dead body. That image will stay with me forever.

> *When you step away from the "write what you know" rule, research becomes inevitable, and it can add a lot to your story. Just don't end up with the tail wagging the dog: remember that you are writing a novel, not a research paper. The story always comes first.*—Stephen King

A final word about the proper use of research. Many years ago I co-wrote a novel called *1919: The Love Letters of George and Adelaide*. My co-writer and I spent many long hours at our respective university libraries reading old newspapers on microfiche, a thoroughly dispiriting activity, but by the time we started writing we were filled to the brim with facts about Canada from the moment the armistice was signed in 1918 to the end of the year 1919.

Our editor was not impressed. "Your research is drawing attention to itself," he said. "A good steak is marbled with fat that brings flavour to the meat; good writing is marbled with research that brings flavour to the piece. Your research is a glob of fat in the middle of your narrative. Your readers will want to spit it out, and I don't blame them."

Make your research an integral part of your novel, enhancing its flavour and deepening its meaning. Use research wisely, and you will be rewarded both professionally and personally. As a writer, you will gain a solid base upon which to build your fictional world. As a human being, you will discover the truth in Hamlet's words: "There are more things in heaven and earth . . . than are dreamt of in your philosophy."

ENGLISH 100 REDUX

Take out the five mystery novels you've most enjoyed, and sharpen your pencils. Analyze the books you're reading as if you were back in English 100, keeping one particular question in mind: Why?

1. Why did the writer choose this narrative perspective? If he chose first person, why did he choose to write from this particular character's perspective? Would the writer's purpose be better served if events were seen through the eyes of a different character? Did his choice work or not work?
2. Why this setting? Why this location? Why this time of year? If the action moves from place to place, why does it move? If most of the novel centres on one particular setting, why did the writer choose to keep his focus narrow? Why did his choices work or not work?
3. Why this protagonist? Why did the writer make the choices he made about revealing the character of his protagonist? (Is the character revealed through actions? words? thoughts? relationships? words and thoughts of others?) And–yet again–why did his choices work or not work?
4. Why did the writer choose this particular gallery of secondary characters? Are they fully realized?

In a well-written novel, every character serves a purpose (more about this later). Is the function of each secondary character clear in this novel? Why or why not?

5. If we define plot as "what happens" and structure as "the order in which what happens is presented to the reader," has the writer told us what happens as effectively as possible? Does the plot lag anywhere? Does it make sense? Is the pacing of plot points effective? Does the structure serve the plot? Why?
6. Look at the openings of those five mysteries that knocked your socks off. Notice how often they begin *in medias res*—"in the middle of things"—with an ongoing situation that draws you in and makes you want to turn the page. Your grandmother was right: you never get a second chance to make a first impression. Don't blow it! Remember always that the writer's first task is to keep the reader reading. How do the openings of the novels you're exploring hook you?
7. Why do the five books you chose conclude as they do? It's a given that at the end of a mystery the murderer must be brought to justice, and the motivation for the murder and the strategies by which the murderer committed the act and by which (for a time at least) he evaded detection must be made clear. That said, to paraphrase Dr. Seuss's Grinch musing about the meaning of Christmas, what if the denouement is "something more" than a simple tying together of loose ends? What if it is the place where the writer offers the reader an insight into the complex business of living a life?

As you sit down to write, reflect on what you learned from the English 100 Redux exercise. How can the choices of the writers you admire help you to shape your own writing and create work with your own stamp? Give yourself plenty of time to make your decisions. Remember the old carpenter's axiom: "Measure twice, cut once."

MAPPING YOUR NOVEL

> *I always know the end of the mystery before I begin to write. Tension should be held within the novel, and there should be no longueurs of boring interrogation.*—P. D. James

When I do a Q&A after a reading, one question I'm invariably asked is whether I work from a detailed outline or just make a start and let my imagination take flight. It's a fair question. I know crime fiction writers who fill the walls of their workrooms with note cards detailing each scene in each chapter. I also know others who simply follow their muses.

My process is somewhere in the middle. Mysteries are plot driven. They give the reader a story, and mysteries have always had a fair-play rule. The reader's opportunity to solve the mystery must be equal to the detective's opportunity. And for me that means the writer must have control of his or her material.

In a good mystery, there is always the "aha" moment. When the lion asks the fox why he doesn't follow the example of the other animals by entering the lion's den, and the fox says "I see many footprints going into your den but none coming out," that is the "aha" moment for both the fox and the reader. For me, giving the reader this moment means I have to know before I begin writing who the killer is, who the victim is, and why the murder is committed.

Rather than blather on in abstractions, I'm going to risk my publisher's ire and illustrate the point with specifics from my sixteenth Joanne Kilbourn novel, *What's Left Behind.* The victim is Lee Crawford, a striking thirty-three-year old farmer continuing the breeding of heritage animals that was the lifelong work of Colin Brokenshire, the man who raised Lee and her identical twin, Maisie, after their parents were killed in a car accident. The murderer is Bette Stevens, a strong and attractive farmer in her late fifties who has been a presence in the lives of Lee and Maisie since Colin became their legal guardian. Bette and Colin had a relationship that ended when Colin and Lee fell in love. When Colin told Bette he and Lee were planning to marry, Bette killed him in what appeared to be a farm accident. Eleven years later, when Bette's son Bobby tells his mother Lee has accepted his proposal of marriage, Bette kills Lee.

As P. D. James says, "A first class mystery should also be a first class novel." The fact that I know not only the identity of the murderer but also her motivation gives me a strong foundation upon which to build when I turn to developing characters and their relationships, writing individual scenes, and working out the plot and its subplots–in short, when I begin writing the novel.

CHAPTER 4

WRITING YOUR MYSTERY

What good is a poet/What good is this pen, this yellow paper, if I can't fashion them into tools or weapons to change our lives?—Beth Brant

YOUR GOAL IN WRITING

Beth Brant's haunting lines point to what I suggested earlier should be the first question all writers ask themselves: "What do I hope to accomplish with this piece of writing?" If your goal is to bring readers diversion and pleasure, and you have written a solid, absorbing novel that keeps them turning the pages until they close your book with a satisfied sigh, then you've done your work. If, however, your answer, like Brant's question, involves enlarging readers' minds and/or moving readers to action, then you must ask yourself a few more questions. "Is there something I want to say here about human nature, human conduct, and the business of living?" "What's the big idea behind my novel or story?" "What is my thesis?" "What is my theme?"

Never lose sight of the fact that storytelling is a vehicle for human connection. When your theme runs beneath your writing like the figured bass in a fugue, your characters gain depth and resonance, and your plot line becomes clearer and more intense. When your reader puts down your novel thinking that her mind has been enlarged by her connection with you, then you've done your job as a writer.

Just as knowing the identities of the murderer and the victim and understanding why the murder was committed give you a solid structure upon which to build a novel that satisfies the reader who seeks diversion and pleasure, so too knowing the "big idea" behind your novel will help you to keep your theme in focus as you write. It will also save you tons of time and endless frustration.

For a writer, there is no darker moment than the one in which you realize that the effervescent idea you've been pursuing has taken you nowhere and, worse yet, is about to burst. But the questions "What is the big idea behind my story or novel?" and "What is my thesis or theme?" not only give you solid ground on which to begin but can also be useful diagnostic tools when you go astray.

If you're confronted with a piece of writing that suddenly seems—like Stephen Leacock's famous horseman—to be riding madly off in all directions, then go back to your beginning point. Retrace your path, and discover where you lost sight of your theme or thesis.

> *Don't sit down in the middle of the woods. If you're lost in the plot or blocked, retrace your steps to where you went wrong. Then take the other road. And/or change the person. Change the tense. Change the opening page.*—Margaret Atwood

I'm going to use *What's Left Behind* as an example of the importance of remembering at all times what you hope to achieve with your work. When I was writing the first draft of *What's Left Behind*, I had problems keeping the theme in sharp focus, and I had to relearn some lessons. These lessons, of course, are ones I've taught students of writing for years but apparently forgot to listen to myself.

Here's one nugget of wisdom that seemingly slipped my mind. Decide on the right title for your novel as early in the process as possible. Charles Dickens is said to have chosen the title *Bleak House* before he wrote a word of the novel. I can't remember how many titles I tried out before I finally hit on *What's Left Behind*, but the *fluffiness* (there's that word again) of the early drafts was reflected in the fact that I continued to struggle for a title when I was well into writing the book.

Canadian novelist Alastair MacLeod says, "Writers write about what worries them." One thing that has become an increasingly acute worry for me in the past fifteen years is urban sprawl, the creeping blight that threatens so much of our agricultural land and the sense of community in our cities. Few elected representatives or officials seem to be prepared to seriously examine the untrammelled civic growth that leaves a poisonous legacy for generations to come. I wanted to write about that, and I wanted to deal with the troubling undercurrent of irrationality running through contemporary political life. I knew what I wanted to say, but I wasn't clear on how exactly I was going to say it. As soon as I settled on the title *What's Left Behind*, I was able to see the problem and deal with it.

The title *What's Left Behind* resonates on two levels. The novel opens on a May morning so perfect Joanne believes it merits a haiku. She and her husband, Zack, the mayor of Regina, are preparing for their son Peter's marriage to Maisie Crawford, a woman wholeheartedly embraced by Peter's family. Maisie's maid of honour is her twin sister, Lee, who sees herself as a steward of the land she owns and is actively supporting Zack's campaign to pass a referendum on a set of bylaws ensuring that the city's future development is carefully planned and respectful of rural land that has been used for farming for generations.

When the fight over the referendum leads first to the poisoning of Lee's prized heritage poultry and later to her murder, questions are raised about the kind of world we, as a society, want to leave behind. Our ethical and environmental decisions will shape our children and their inheritance. What kind of people will they become? What will they inherit?

The fact that the murder victim is someone close to Joanne's family brings the title's second level of meaning to the forefront. The sudden death of a loved one leaves those who remain struggling to discover how they can use the fragments of the life that's left behind after the death to build a new life that will have purpose and beauty.

The title *What's Left Behind* is a signal to my readers that I was in control of my material—that the killing of Lee's prized birds isn't simply a plot point. The wanton slaughter of the poultry reveals the ugliness humans can be driven to when their goals are thwarted, and it foreshadows the murder to come. As well, in irreparably severing a link to the past, the killing of the birds underscores the novel's theme that what's done cannot always be undone.

A final note about titles. The title the writer chooses while working on the manuscript is known, not surprisingly, as the "working title," and you should prepare yourself for the possibility that your working title is not necessarily the title that will appear on your book's glossy cover when it reaches the bookseller.

The final titles of three of the eighteen Joanne Kilbourn mysteries were not their working titles. The first novel, *Deadly Appearances*, was originally titled "Murder in the Granny Flat." My publishers thought that title gave away too much of the plot and replaced it with the somewhat generic title it has borne for almost three decades. *A Colder Kind of Death* was the choice of James Adams, my first M&S editor and now the visual arts editor of the *Globe and Mail*. We were floundering for a title, and he came up with *A Colder Kind of Death*. It works well with the novel, and I loved it from the start. The eighteenth Joanne Kilbourn mystery started out as "The Other Self," but my publishers weren't wild about my choice, so when I suggested *A Darkness of the Heart* they jumped for joy.

A USEFUL IF APOCRYPHAL STORY

At least five people in the book business have told me this story; I can't vouch for its truthfulness, but it makes a valid point.

An up-and-coming writer has an appointment with a famous agent. The agent's office is on the fifty-eighth floor of a building in downtown Toronto (or Vancouver or New York City, depending on the teller of the tale). By coincidence, the writer and the agent step into the elevator at the same time. After a quick introduction, the agent says, "Tell me what your novel's about." The writer murbles and burbles in generalities until the elevator reaches the fifty-eighth floor. When the writer attempts to follow the agent out of the elevator, she raises her hand in a "halt" gesture. "Push the down button," she says. "If you don't know what your novel's about, you're not worth my time."

The story might be apocryphal, but its moral is clear. If a writer can't state in one sentence (or two at the most) what she is hoping to communicate through a piece of writing, she needs to rethink her piece.

Literature moves from the particular to the universal. As a writer, your job is to develop your themes through fully rounded characters whose actions and dialogue reveal thematic patterns for your reader to discover. Make your world real, and you can explore the great themes.

Before we move on to the in-depth exploration of how you can most effectively use the elements of fiction to connect with your reader, a quick overview of some tips to manage your writing process might be useful.

1. Write every day, even if it's only for fifteen minutes or to jot something down in your notebook or to do a quick edit on your work from the day before. Day-by-day engagement with your work keeps the connection alive and the juices flowing.
2. Never leave your writing in a bad spot. If you know a quagmire awaits you, the temptation *not* to go back to your laptop can be almost irresistible. Some of my best writing moments have come after I've gritted my teeth and stayed at my laptop till I've worked through the problem. Ernest Hemingway said, "Always leave the pump primed." It's good advice. And novelist Jodi Picoult tartly observed, "You

can edit a bad page, but you can't edit a blank page." If you're in what a writer friend of mine refers to as "suck mode," then the process will be painful, but take a few deep breaths and forge ahead.

3. Many writers, and I am among them, believe that two quiet hours at 5 A.M. equal four hours of regular work time. Ignore this advice if you are a night owl.
4. When you're stuck, leave your desk. Go for a walk. Make tea. Play with your dog or cat. Meditate. Whatever you do, don't start surfing the net, don't make a phone call, and don't get together with friends. If you do, other people's words will pour in where your words should be. Create a space for your words. Be patient.
5. Use the Pomodoro Technique. Work for twenty-five minutes. Give yourself a five-minute break, and then get back to work. I've been doing this since I started writing. Until a couple of years ago, I had no idea this particular strategy had a name, but it does, and by any name the technique works.
6. Trust your instincts. If a character begins to surprise you, follow him to see where he takes you. In *12 Rose Street*, I have a character who is a slumlord and an enthusiastic proponent of rough sex. He is reptilian in appearance, and after a bitter battle with his father he had his birth name legally changed from Harvey Mewhort Jr. to Cronus to suggest his affinity with the ruling Titan in Greek mythology who came to power by castrating his father Uranus. Cronus is an unlikely hero, yet, when he is faced with a decision to risk his own life or the life of a child, he chooses to risk himself and pays the price.

7. Trust your instincts even when you don't want to. Sometimes, despite your best efforts, a character is lifeless, a plot line is limp, a symbol is leaden, or, horror of horrors, your whole manuscript has the vitality of a long-dead mackerel. Give that draft of the manuscript a decent burial and start again. Try some creative recycling of the characters and plot points that didn't work in the first draft. You might be amazed at how they snap, crackle, and pop the second time around. Remember P. D. James's wise counsel: "Nothing is ever wasted."
8. Never give up.
9. Learn to be your own editor. I begin every day rewriting the last page or so I wrote the day before. I always find something to shift or change. And working on the familiar material helps me to reconnect with the manuscript and gets the juices running again.
10. E. L. Doctorow said that writing "is like driving a car at night: you can never see further than your headlights, but you can make the whole trip that way." Keep the faith.

CHAPTER 5

POINT OF VIEW/ NARRATIVE PERSPECTIVE

To put this most simply, point of view is merely a decision the writer makes that will determine through whose eyes the story is going to be told.—Elizabeth George, author of the Inspector Thomas Lynley mysteries

Six of my novels have been made into movies, and I have watched with respect the care taken to cast each role. The casting director goes through literally hundreds of actors' resumes, culls most of them, and then chooses the actors who will be called in for a test. These actors are asked to read scenes alone and with other actors. The process is repeated until those ultimately responsible for producing the movie decide that they have found the actors who can best bring the screenplay's characters to life.

Casting the right actor for a role is a rigorous procedure. Writers must be equally rigorous in deciding which narrative voice and perspective will best serve their novels. Take your time. Try writing a scene from different points of view. Try it in the first person. Try it with several different first-person narrators. Try it in third-person subjective. Or try it with an omniscient narrator. Then consider which method of narration felt the most natural for you and which allowed you to communicate most effectively what you wanted to say.

FIRST PERSON

The story is told through the eyes of one person using the pronoun *I*. I've used a first-person narrator for both the Joanne Kilbourn series and the Charlie Dowhanuik series. I've also used first person for one novella and one very short piece. It's a good fit for me. I like getting inside a character's head, and I like imagining what life must look like through her or his eyes. It's a personal call, and I seem to slip into it easily, but it might not be for you.

Trust your instincts. The one time I've used third-person narrative was for "The Foad Toad," a comic short story I wrote for *University Affairs*. It focused on a male professor in late middle age who couldn't or wouldn't adjust to the tectonic shifts in university culture that had occurred over the past fifteen years. I began the story using a first-person narrator, but I quickly shifted to third-person narration. The protagonist, Phineas, is a sympathetic character, but I realized that it was important for the point I wanted to make that the reader not see the university wholly through his eyes.

That said, there are times when a first-person narrator is just what the doctor ordered. Remember Ms. X from Banff? She was a charming woman with a beautiful contralto voice and the kind of energy that warmed a chilly room. There was nothing technically amiss in the manuscript she gave me. Everything that needed to be established was established, but the piece was grey and lifeless.

When Ms. X and I talked about the problem, I was struck again by the force of her personality. As is often the case, there was a character in her draft much like her. I suggested to Ms. X that she rewrite a few pages in the first person using the point of view of that character. The revised piece pulsed with colour and life. Ms. X had found her character's voice, and that voice brought her story to life.

Take a few narrative perspectives out for a spin. You'll know when you've found the one that works best for you.

Advantage of First-Person Narrative

First-person narrative is a powerful tool if the mystery you're writing is character driven. Because readers see everything through the eyes of the narrator-protagonist, they come to know your protagonist intimately. The reader is privy to the protagonist's thoughts, opinions, emotions, and reactions. Reader and narrator form a bond. The fact that information is revealed to the reader as it is revealed to the narrator creates a sense of immediacy that further strengthens that bond. Yet, because everything the reader knows is filtered through the lens of the narrator-protagonist, the reader never sees the complete picture, never has all the information. The reader has only the narrator's perception of what others are doing.

That said, as readers we have double vision. We are inside the head of the narrator-protagonist when we read, but when we reflect on what we are reading our thoughts are our own. We form our own judgments, and they might differ from those formed by the first-person narrator.

If the writer is in control of his material, then he can use this double vision to show that the perceptions of his protagonist are flawed. She could be unwittingly blinded by love or past history. In this case, double vision allows us, as readers, to glimpse the truth and to gain a new perspective on the narrator-protagonist.

Canadian writer Sinclair Ross uses the double vision perspective to stunning effect in his novel *As for Me and My House.* The entire novel is written as a diary kept by a preacher's wife during the dirty thirties in Saskatchewan. In her diary, Mrs. Bentley—we never know her given name—presents herself as a loving wife who sacrifices herself willingly for her husband. When he repays her selflessness by impregnating a woman in the church choir and the woman dies in childbirth, Mrs. Bentley welcomes the newborn baby to their family.

We see everything and everyone through the eyes of this first-person narrator, and at first glance Mrs. Bentley seems to be a paragon. However, a careful reading of the novel shows a darker side of Ross's narrator-protagonist. When Mrs. Bentley says of her marriage "I hollowed myself out so that I might enclose him," I felt a chill, and when I reread the book I saw that the narrator's own words reveal a much darker Mrs. Bentley, a woman who believes that the roses on her wallpaper are like eyes, following her and judging her, and that her husband's parishioners deliberately time their visits to catch her with her floors unscrubbed and her dishes unwashed.

Ross uses his readers' double vision to create a layered and compelling protagonist, and *As for Me and My House* is deservedly a classic. In a later chapter, I'll talk about how I use my readers' double vision to show how Joanne Kilbourn's need for acceptance blinds Joanne to the true nature of a character whom she has loved since childhood.

Multiple First-Person Narrators in a Single Novel

Emerging writers frequently ask me about the wisdom of using more than one first-person narrator. I understand the appeal. The threads that bind human beings together in relationships are as complex and fragile as the filaments of a spider's web. It's inevitable that a sensitive writer is drawn to the prospect of probing that web from different first-person perspectives. That said, I invariably advise against the use of more than one first-person narrator simply because, as a rule, juggling two or more narrators is hard and often unrewarding work.

If you are truly committed to using multiple narrators, I recommend that you read Louise Erdrich's novel *The Plague of Doves*. That brilliant novel illustrates both the power and the danger of using multiple narrators. For the most part, Erdrich's use of many voices to tell her tale works well, but the narrator given the responsibility of tying up the loose ends at the conclusion of the novel is weak, and to my mind the ending feels cobbled together. *The Plague of Doves* is a terrific book, but a writer should always finish strong, so there's a lesson in that ending.

When your Grade 6 grammar teacher told you that for every rule there is an exception, she must have been anticipating Gillian Flynn's best-selling novel/blockbuster film *Gone Girl*. Flynn's novel is a breathtaking example of how a skilled writer can use two unreliable narrators to draw the reader into the maelstrom of a marriage gone terribly wrong.

Form and Function

The principle that the shape of a building or an object should be based primarily upon its intended function is associated mostly with architecture; however, the idea that the form of a work of fiction might serve the writer's purpose is a provocative one.

Gone Girl is the autopsy of a marriage both partners are eager to kill. In choosing the warring husband and wife as dual first-person narrators shoving one another out of the way to present the "truth" of their marriage to the reader, Flynn has found the perfect form to serve her novel's function.

Nick, the husband, is the primary storyteller in Part 1. His narration takes us into the events leading up to his wife Amy's disappearance and apparent murder. However, Amy is also present through the journal she leaves behind with her account of "the realities" of her marriage to Nick.

In Part 2, Amy takes centre stage as the first-person narrator, noting that the journal she left behind is a tissue of lies ("I hope you liked Diary Amy. She was meant to be likeable") and revealing her plot to frame Nick. In theatre, the act of addressing the audience directly is called "breaking the fourth wall," and Flynn has both of her unreliable narrators break the fourth wall and make direct appeals to readers in order to get them onside. In attempting to enlist bystanders in their war against each other, Amy and Nick mirror the behaviour of the combatants in many broken marriages. Again Flynn uses the tools she has as a writer to realize her purpose. Art imitates life, and the result is a wrenching portrait of what happens when passionate love sours into something vile.

Choosing a First-Person Narrator

1. Is this the character with whom both you and your readers will be content to spend time?
2. Is this the character who can best explore what you believe to be the truth about the human condition?
3. If your plan is to write a series with this narrator-protagonist, does he or she have the potential to go the distance?

This last is not an idle question. I've known more than one mystery series that ran aground because the writer had simply exhausted the possibilities for the protagonist.

My decision to allow my protagonist Joanne Kilbourn to age wasn't based upon a master plan for a lengthy series. I wanted Joanne to be middle-aged because I was middle-aged, and I'd noticed that middle-aged protagonists were underrepresented in mystery novels. I decided to have Joanne age because I was aging, and I found the process an interesting one.

Ruth Rendell, Baroness Rendell of Babergh, and I once had a spirited moment over that decision during a panel discussion at the Vancouver International Writers and Readers Festival. During the Q&A after our panel, a reader asked me about my decision to allow Joanne to grow older. Before I could answer, the Baroness jumped in, shaking her finger at me. "You'll regret that, my girl," she said.

I have a sense that, in her long and productive life, the late Baroness was not often wrong, but she was mistaken about that. Joanne was forty-three when the series began, and she is now sixty. For her, as for all of us, aging has brought both joy and sadness. Most importantly for the series, age has brought many changes to her life, and in a later chapter I'll discuss how the characters introduced by those changes have given me very rich material with which to work.

I have been asked so frequently if Joanne Kilbourn Shreve is my "alter ego" that I finally looked up the term. According to *Merriam Webster*, "an alter ego can be thought of as a person's clone or second self." The question is a fair one. Joanne and I are both mothers, grandmothers, university professors, occasional media commentators, and political activists. The facts that we both have children, grandchildren, and dogs that we love and that we both live in Lakeview, a beautiful neighbourhood of tree-lined streets and old homes, further muddy the waters. As does the fact that Joanne's "take" on people and institutions is close to my own.

That said, Joanne is not my "clone or second self." As someone who taught Canadian literature for many years, I wanted a protagonist whose character had been shaped by this country and who was deeply committed to making Canada a good place for all of its citizens. As well, I wanted someone who was deeply rooted in her family and community.

> *You write from what you know, but you write into what you don't know.*—Grace Paley

The eighteen Joanne Kilbourn novels have given me approximately 5,580 pages in which to explore my protagonist's character. I know Joanne well, but in writing her I have come to see the wisdom of Grace Paley's observation.

Once, as an exercise, I took a character from *Burying Ariel*, the book I was working on at the time, and had her describe Joanne. It was a useful experiment, and I recommend it to all writers who have decided on a first-person narrator-protagonist. The character I chose to describe Joanne is Solange Levy, a young radical female colleague in the Department of Political Science, where they both teach. I learned a great deal from Solange's opinion of Joanne. "It's tempting to dismiss Joanne," Solange says. "She's so easy to dismiss: middle age, middle height, middle weight, middle class, intellect at the middle of the scale, with middlebrow interests, but once in awhile she does something extraordinary." Joanne might be just as unexceptional as Solange believes her to be, but like all of us Joanne is more than the sum of her parts. As a character, she continues to surprise me, and the moments when she surprises not only me but also herself are among the most vivid in the series.

American literary theorist Kenneth Burke has suggested that literature can provide "equipment for living." Later in *Sleuth* is a chapter devoted to how secondary characters can be used to illuminate the character of the protagonist. The chapter dwells in depth on Joanne's inner self–on the forces that have shaped Joanne and on her strengths and vulnerabilities. It contains a number of ideas that I believe will be helpful as you create your own characters.

However, for the time being, my focus is on the fact that, in making Joanne as deeply flawed as most of us, I've created a character with whom many readers identify. Occasionally, the events of her life and her reactions to them open a vein of response in readers that makes me realize the profound responsibility that we, as writers, have to our readers.

In *12 Rose Street*, Joanne's husband, Zack, is running for mayor of Regina. The campaign is vicious, and as his campaign manager Joanne is considered a fair target. The opposition approaches Joanne with audio tapes of her late husband, Ian Kilbourn, having sex with her best friend, Jill Oziowy, and gives her an ultimatum: if she doesn't convince Zack to withdraw from the race, the rival campaign will send the tapes to her children. Joanne rejects the offer, and in the following scene she confronts Jill.

> "The kids just found out about you and Ian."
>
> "Oh my God. How did that happen. . . ." [Jill's] sentence trailed off. The full horror of the situation was beginning to hit her. "Jo, we have to talk."
>
> "I agree," I said. "But I don't want to talk here." Still holding her hot dog, Jill followed as I went up the stairs to the stage and back to the green room.
>
> After she closed the door behind her, Jill looked at me beseechingly. "Jo, you have to understand—"
>
> "Shut up," I said. "There's nothing to understand. I may be naïve but I get this. . . . An hour ago I stood in this room and listened while Slater Doyle played an audio tape of you fellating Ian and him returning the favour. The quality of the recording was excellent. I felt as if I

> was in the room with you. And the clip I heard was just a sample. Slater told me the affair began before Mieka was born and was still going on when Ian died."
>
> Jill's entire body was shaking. It was as if she'd been suddenly plunged into ice water. "Jo, please. Give me a chance to make things right. I'll do anything."
>
> "You've done enough," I said. "We're finished. Get your things out of Mieka's house. Then go away and stay away." For a moment my heart went out to her. But the moment didn't last. "Better eat your hot dog," I said. "It's getting cold."

12 Rose Street is the fifteenth book in the series. Readers thought they had come to know Joanne. They knew she believed that when Ian died he was wholly committed to the family he loved. They saw the warmth and mutual support that characterized her friendship with Jill. Joanne's pain, confusion, and rage at the dual betrayal struck a chord with readers. They knew, as Joanne herself did, that the only way she would find peace was through the agonizing but necessary journey to forgiveness.

The number of readers who approached me, either in person or through email, asking me if I could teach them how to forgive was a reminder of a first-person narrator's power to connect with readers. It also underscored the fact that as writers we must always be mindful of the fact that the stories we tell bind us to those who read our books.

The "Watson" Narrator

Named for Dr. John Watson, the narrator of Sir Arthur Conan Doyle's Sherlock Holmes stories, this narrator is the assistant closest to the principal sleuth. Such narrators are integral parts of the action. In revealing events as they occur, these narrators give readers the sense that reader and detective are uncovering evidence together. Equally importantly, they also give readers ongoing and sometimes critical observations about the big guy. Theirs are the voices we hear when we read the novels.

Here's Archie Goodwin in *The Silent Speaker* on his boss:

> Wolfe was in bed. Wolfe in bed was always a remarkable sight, accustomed to it as I was. First the low bootboard, of streaky anselmo; yellowish with sweeping dark brown streaks; then the black silk coverlet, next the wide expanse of yellow pyjama top, and last the flesh of the face. In my opinion Wolfe was quite aware that black and yellow are a flashy combination, and he used it deliberately just to prove that no matter how showy the scene was he could dominate it. I have often thought I would like to see him try it with pink and green.

And Dr. Watson in *The Adventures of the Creeping Man* on his boss:

> Holmes was a man of habits . . . and I had become one of them . . . a comrade . . .

> upon whose nerve he could place some reliance . . . a whetstone for his mind. I stimulated him. . . . If I irritated him by a certain methodical slowness in my mentality, that irritation served only to make his own flame-like intuitions and impressions flash up the more vividly and swiftly. Such was my humble role in our alliance.

SECOND PERSON

In second-person narrative, the narrator refers to him- or herself as "you" in a way that suggests alienation from the events described. Alternatively, the author addresses the reader directly as "you."

It's rarely used. Offhand, I can think of only one book I've actually read that uses it: Jay McInerney's slick and immensely successful debut novel *Bright Lights, Big City* (1984). In it, the unnamed narrator offers readers a play-by-play account of his life spinning out of control when he is on a bender:

> The night has already turned on that imperceptible pivot where two A.M. changes to six A.M. . . . Somewhere back there you could have cut your losses, but you rode past that moment on a comet trail of white powder and now you are trying to hang on to the rush. Your brain at this moment is composed of brigades of tiny Bolivian soldiers. They are tired and muddy from their long march through

> the night. There are holes in their boots
> and they are hungry. They need to be fed.

I can't see second person working well for a crime novel, but if the prospect appeals to you check out that novel, because McInerney handles it well.

THIRD PERSON

In third-person narrative, the narrator refers to every character in the third person: that is, either by given names or as "he," "she," or "they." The narrator is unspecified and is not a character within the story. Third-person narration gives the writer the greatest flexibility of any narrative mode, and for that reason it is used most frequently.

Flexibility

In third-person narration, the writer is not confined to a single point of view. She is free to move through time and space, and can know what drives every character to do what they do.

American police procedural writer Richard Price has been justly praised for his dialogue and his mastery of the rhythms of everyday speech. In addition to his crime novels, Price has written screenplays and co-written TV series, including *The Wire* and *The Night Of*. In his novel *Lush Life*, the advantages of third-person narration are apparent.

A friend who is an appeals court judge told me once that most murders are sad, unpremeditated, wrong place/wrong time incidents. *Lush Life* deals with the aftermath of one such murder. The victim, Ike Marcus, an aspiring writer/probationary bartender, goes out drinking with his supervisor, Eric Cash, and Steven Boulware, another probationary bartender. Headed for home, they are confronted by three teenage boys from the projects who demand their money. Boulware passes out, Cash hands over his wallet, but Marcus refuses, saying "Not tonight, my man." He is shot to death. One of the first cops on the scene calls his death "suicide by mouth." *Lush Life* has a large cast of characters: the police investigating the murder, the grieving family of the victim, the shooters, their families, and their acquaintances in the projects.

Third-person narration allows Price to follow the lives and thoughts of at least a score of these characters, and he makes them come to life as people we know and care about. Such narration also allows him to give us a sense of the very different worlds his characters inhabit and how they have been shaped by those worlds. When the shooter is identified and brought to police headquarters for an interview, Price describes his attitude in a single sentence that captures the inevitability of the young man's tragic destiny:

> The kid seemed unbreakable; as in, broken so many times there was nothing left to break; coming off as if he were sitting in the back row of a meaningless class, barely interested in his own lying answers to where he had been that night, as to how he came upon the gun found under his mattress; indifferent to the point of boredom to all the contradictions pointed out to him in his narrative; indifferent to his own fate.

Tension

Writers working with first-person narration will hit certain "dead spaces" where events might be transpiring, but the narrator is not yet aware of them. Third-person narration allows the reader to be aware of everything that's going on and keeps the pace brisk. Readers of *Lush Life* can be aware of how the investigation is progressing while they continue to follow the lives and thoughts of the police on the case, of the grieving father and his family, and of the shooter and his circle of friends. Moving from one character to another creates momentum.

Third-person narration allows the writer to show what drives the antagonist and what drives the protagonist. It allows the writer to heighten suspense by tracking the inexorable movement of antagonist and protagonist toward each other.

Distance

For writers considering writing about their own experiences or those of someone close to them, third-person narration allows them to distance themselves from material that might be inherently painful or constricting. Frequently, I have suggested using the third person to students who, in telling their stories, found themselves blocked by their emotions or concerns for others.

CHAPTER 6

SETTING

The world a writer writes about is not chosen accidentally. Most often a writer chooses a fictional world that allows her/him to say best what s/he believes is true of the human condition.—Robert Penn Warren

American novelist and literary critic Robert Penn Warren cites Ernest Hemingway's belief that it is only by facing down death every day that a man (and for Hemingway it was *always* about the man) can live his life fully. Warren illustrates his theory that setting is integral to communicating theme by pointing to some of the places where Hemingway chose to set his novels: a war zone, a bullfight ring, a small boat carrying a man alone on the ocean. If you're keen to test the theory further, ponder Jane Austen's famous line: "It is a truth universally acknowledged that a single man in possession of a good fortune must be in want of a wife." Think of the exquisitely drawn cameo of Austen's fictional world. Can you imagine a Hemingway hero nibbling a scone at a vicarage tea party or, conversely, an Austen heroine sidling up to a bullfighter?

The care with which writers of crime fiction choose the fictional world that allows them to say best what they believe is true of the human condition is apparent in all mysteries but particularly in mystery series. On the streets of Watts, where—fifty years after the 1968 riots—rage and resentment still smoulder, Walter Mosley, author of the Ezekiel "Easy" Rawlins series, found a world that shows what poverty, alienation, racism, and hopelessness do to human beings. In the Arcadian beauty of Three Pines in Quebec's Eastern Townships, Louise Penny (the Armand Gamache series) created a community that offers an antidote to the conviction that the world is a cruel and dangerous place, a belief that was part of the collateral damage of 9/11. In the underbelly of Chicago, a place of almost Dickensian darkness, Sara Paretsky (the V.I. Warshawski series) found a canvas that allows her to show that, in our most shining and affluent cities, if you have the bad luck to be born poor, female, black, Hispanic, or challenged physically, intellectually, or emotionally, you might be consigned to a life that is nasty, brutish, and often short.

I could go on, but the point is clear: in crime fiction, setting is not simply backdrop; it is a crucial element of the novel and a key factor not only in establishing the reader's loyalty to the series but also in deepening the reader's understanding of the novel's characters.

WRITING IN REGINA

I live in Regina, the capital city of Saskatchewan, the only Canadian province shaped like a rectangle. The population of Regina varies, but generally it hovers around 230,000. Regina is a city that most people drive through to get somewhere else. At first blush, it does not appear to offer much to write about.

In Julian Barnes's novel *The Sense of an Ending*, the protagonist relates what he believed about literature when he was a young man. "Literature," he says, "was all about: love, sex, morality, friendship, happiness, suffering, betrayal, adultery, good and evil, heroes and villains, guilt and innocence, ambition, power, justice, revolution, war, fathers and sons, mothers and daughters, the individual against society, success and failure, murder, suicide, death, God."

Interviewers regularly ask me if the fact that I set my novels in Saskatchewan limits their sales. Of course, I have no way of knowing, but I do know that, like every hamlet, village, town, or city where human beings live, Regina has enough of what Barnes's protagonist notes to fill a good-sized library with books.

Even more significantly, Regina has allowed me to say what I believe is true about the human condition. I believe we are all part of a community, and for that reason, among many, we should be quick to empathize and slow to judge. I believe social issues such as poverty, racism, child prostitution, alienation, hopelessness, and spousal violence are issues that we, as a community, must address. As a province with a long tradition of social activism, Saskatchewan was a good fit for my protagonist, Joanne Kilbourn Shreve.

She is not by occupation or inclination a risk taker or windmill tilter. She is acutely aware, however, of the world around her, and she sees many things in her community that worry her. There are just over 1 million people in our province, so we are accustomed to working together to do what needs to be done. Joanne's life, like the lives of many people in Saskatchewan, is informed by the belief that, when ordinary people are confronted by inequity or injustice, they must roll up their sleeves and do what they can to right the wrong. There is plenty to be done, but Joanne's ethos, like my own, can be stated simply: in a flawed but basically decent society, a person of ordinary intelligence and common sense can work within the system and bring about change.

Regina offers me the perfect canvas on which to work. What about you? Look again at those five crime fiction novels you selected earlier as among your favourites. What are their respective writers saying about the complex business of being alive? Why have they selected their particular settings ? Do their selections work for them? Now think about your choice. What world can you create that will allow you to best say what you believe is true about the human condition?

WRITING ABOUT WEATHER

> *Never open a book with weather.*—Elmore Leonard

> *Three rules for mystery writing. Put weather in. Put weather in. Put weather in.*—Joseph Hansen, author of the Dave Brandstetter mysteries

When it comes to admiration for Elmore Leonard, I am second to none, but I'm with Joseph Hansen on the question of weather in crime fiction. Check out the opening of Raymond Chandler's 1938 short story "Red Wind" to see how, by selecting brief but telling details about weather and its effect on character, a writer can establish a world and a mood that draw the reader into the work:

> There was a desert wind blowing that night. It was one of those hot dry Santa Anas that come down through the mountain passes and curl your hair and make your nerves jump and your skin itch. On nights like that every booze party ends in a fight. Meek little wives feel the edge of the carving knife and study their husbands' necks. Anything can happen. You can even get a full glass of beer at a cocktail lounge.

It's a brilliant opening, one that I've used in creative writing classes to encourage students to establish the mood of a piece by showing the effect weather can have on people.

I once asked a writers' group in Calgary to use Chandler's opening as a model for opening a story about events that take place in their city during a chinook, that warm, dry wind in winter that comes down from the eastern slopes of the Rockies and causes a rapid rise in temperature. I've never experienced a chinook, but whenever I've heard on the news about a chinook passing through Calgary I've assumed the sudden influx of mild weather in the midst of frigid winter would be a welcome gift. Not so. Apparently, during a chinook, there's a sharp rise in aberrant behaviour. Migraine sufferers are hit hard, psychiatric wards are filled, and police are run ragged. My students' riveting descriptions of the effects of a chinook drew me into their stories and kept me reading. That, of course, is exactly what a story opening is supposed to do.

Saskatchewan licence plates carry the motto "Land of the Living Skies." The words capture both the beauty and the uncertainty of living on the open prairie with its constant reminder that human beings are very small and the sky is very large.

The following passage from *The Wandering Soul Murders*, the third Joanne Kilbourn novel, describes a northern Saskatchewan lake so huge it creates its own weather. In order to rescue her young daughter from a sexual predator, Joanne is forced to enlist an unlikely ally, a man named Jackie Desjarlais. The strange and menacing setting terrifies her, and all five senses are on full alert. The first voice we hear in this scene is that of Desjarlais.

> "Let's go," he said. "My boat's down at the dock. You got money for gas? I drank my last five bucks."
>
> "I've got money," I said, and I handed what I had to him.
>
> When he came back, Jackie had a gas can and a bottle of rye. His boat was a new one. Fiberglass, with a fifty-horsepower outboard motor. It looked sturdy. Then I looked out at Havre Lake, and suddenly the boat seemed very small. Jackie reached under the bow and pulled out a khaki slicker.
>
> "Put this on," he said. He opened the rye. "Take a slug." I did. The whiskey

> burned my throat, but it warmed and calmed me.
>
> It took us forty-five minutes to get to the island, forty-five minutes of being pounded by the storm and my own fear. We were heading into the wind, and the rain was blinding. Every time Jackie's boat slapped against the whitecaps, it shuddered as if it was about to split in two. My panic hit in waves, overwhelming me. At one point, I looked out and I couldn't see anything: no island, no shoreline, no line dividing earth from heaven. In that moment I felt a stab of existential terror. I was alone in a frail boat with a stranger. It was a metaphor the psalmist would have understood.

I don't have to describe Joanne's fear; I can show it by noting her reaction to the situation with all five senses—sight, hearing, taste, touch, and smell.

Showing your character's sensory reactions to a scene allows your readers not simply to "see" the setting but also to feel it in their bones. Think for a moment of that scene in the morgue that my police officer friend told me about. The reader's eyes can *see* that the pathologist in charge is performing an autopsy on a very young child. The reader's eyes can *see* that the off-duty pathologist, who came in simply to be with the little boy during his last moments on earth, is standing by the table stroking the child's leg. The picture is poignant.

Now add the responses of the other senses to the scene. The meat-locker cold air. The faint smell of formaldehyde evoking memories of lab dissections of frogs in university biology. The memory of the rough humour of the university labs—a sharp contrast to the reverent silence with which the pathologists approach the child on the autopsy table. The low, comforting murmur of the off-duty pathologist and the unbearable rasp of a surgical instrument sawing through a child's rib cage. The sight of the sign, standard in spaces where autopsies are performed: "This the place where death rejoices to help those who live."

Whether the setting you're describing is a hospital laboratory used for postmortems or the inside of a jalopy where a young man and a young woman are both about to lose their virginity, the judicious use of sensory detail will make the moment come alive.

A final note on setting. At the heart of many long-running mystery series is the home where the protagonist and often his partner in detection work and live. The dwelling can be an elegant brownstone, an apartment, a loft, a Georgian townhouse, or a pleasantly proportioned single-storey house overlooking a pretty creek. For both the protagonist and the reader, this place is the still point in the storm: an oasis for reflection, deduction, and renewal. It is home—a reminder that, after the case has been solved and justice meted out, order will once again prevail, and life will continue.

Think carefully before you choose your fictional world. Not only will the right choice allow you to say what you believe is true about the human condition, but also it will become a place that has real meaning for readers. The following two passages about homes of famous fictional detectives underscore the point.

> On a partly sunny Saturday in June, 1996,
> some 35 members of The Wolfe Pack

descended on 454 West 35th Street to put to rest forever the controversy over exactly where Mr. Wolfe drank beer, raised orchids, ate breakfast, lunch, and dinner, and—oh, yes!—occasionally solved a murder. Commissioner Henry Stern, Department of Parks and Recreation, City of New York dedicated the site.

The plaque reads:

"On this site stood the elegant brownstone of the corpulent fictional private detective Nero Wolfe. With his able assistant Archie Goodwin, Mr. Wolfe raised orchids and dined well, while solving over seventy cases as recorded by Rex Stout from 1934–1975."

The Sherlock Holmes Museum is a privately run museum in London, England, dedicated to the famous fictional detective Sherlock Holmes. It opened in 1990 and is situated in Baker Street, bearing the number 221B by permission of the City of Westminster, although it lies between numbers 237 and 241, near the north end of Baker Street in central London close to Regent's Park.

The Georgian town house which the museum occupies as "221B Baker Street" was formerly used as a boarding house from 1860 to 1936, and covers the period of 1881 to 1904 when Sherlock Holmes and Doctor Watson were reported to have resided there as tenants of Mrs Hudson.

As someone who left her office—an exact replica of the study where Sir Arthur Conan Doyle wrote the Sherlock Holmes mysteries—at the Toronto Reference Library every afternoon while I was the writer-in-residence there, I can attest to the loyalty of readers of crime fiction. Every day at 1 P.M. Sherlockians from all over the world waited patiently to visit the replica of the room where Sherlock Holmes and Dr. Watson came into being. The fans didn't seem to mind the fact that the Conan Doyle study at the Toronto Reference Library wasn't the real thing. They were there to honour Sherlock Holmes.

Mystery aficionados are both the most forgiving and the least forgiving of readers. They will excuse the occasional thin characterization, sketchy setting, improbability or even impossibility, but heaven help the writer who kills off his hero. After Holmes's apparent death at Moriarty's hands in "The Final Problem," public pressure forced Conan Doyle to bring back his sleuth and explain his miraculous survival. Writers planning a long-running series should take note.

CHAPTER 7

CHARACTERIZATION

I didn't care whether the mystery was fairly obvious, but I cared about the people, about this strange corrupt world we live in.
—Raymond Chandler

Good characterization is good characterization, no matter the genre. A satisfying fictional character has dimension, believability, passions, strengths, weaknesses, a degree of self-knowledge, and curiosity about the world around him or her.

Recently, Michael Connelly, author of the Harry Bosch crime novel series, wrote about the changing face of the crime novel:

> The crime novel, in its most serious form, has always been used to reflect trends and lament losses and clang the bell of warning to the ills of society. In a good-versus-evil world the painstaking and dangerous steps of the undaunted

> investigator were the things that riveted the reader while the clever author slipped the message in with the prose. Raymond Chandler said, "Down these mean streets a man must go who is not himself mean, who is neither tarnished nor afraid."
>
> Untarnished and unafraid is easy. But where are those mean streets today? Detective work has changed dramatically in the past quarter-century as science has seemingly replaced shoe leather. Investigators are more likely to solve a case with a walk to the forensics lab than down the mean streets where a murder has occurred. Greatly improved collection of fingerprint and ballistic evidence and their attendant and ever-growing databases routinely ferret out the guilty—or at least the accused.
>
> And then there is DNA. . . . DNA has become the magic bullet, the slam dunk used by prosecutors to leverage the guilty plea that avoids the trial.

Technology has transformed the methods of crime detection, but later in the review Connelly notes that "The steady beating heart of the novel is provided by the criminal psychologist Trajan Jones, late of the New York City Police Department."

Despite all of the changes in the genre, a mystery novel will always require a "steady beating heart" at its centre, and such a heart will always be found in "rounded" characters who engage our interest because of their words, their actions, and their attitudes toward everything from poutine to Puccini.

The sleuth, professional or reluctant, will be surrounded by a gallery of characters, good and bad, different in almost every respect but linked by the fact that, like every other human being, each of them wants *something*, and the pursuit of that nebulous something drives their actions.

In addition to writing fiction, I write plays, and in theatre at the first rehearsal we identify what each character wants more than anything—his or her super-objective. If the writing is solid, then the super-objective will be apparent. The super-objective can change in the course of the play or novel, but the reasons for the change must be apparent to the audience. As Michael Connelly says, "All persons are defined by their wants and needs. Their desires. Attaining the things we want creates conflict within ourselves and in our relations to the world. This natural human condition must be embedded in the people you write about. It helps define their characters. It makes them real." Ray Bradbury puts it more simply: "Find out what your hero wants. Then just follow him." The Bible's insight into this aspect of human nature is both pointed and poetic: "For where your treasure is, there will your heart be also" (Matthew 6:21). Identifying where the "treasure" of each of your characters lies gives you a quick and reliable insight into a character's ambitions and vulnerabilities—a powerful tool when it comes to deciding his or her role in furthering the plot.

One salient point about characters in crime novels: we see them at their worst. Their treasure will be either threatened or taken from them. Their lives will be torn apart. They will suffer actual and existential loss. They will be frightened, bereaved, confused, desperate, and stripped of their masks and their pride. The person they believed themselves to be will be shattered. How they will rebuild their lives and themselves is one of the enduring fascinations of crime fiction.

Interest in the process will be deepened if readers have come to know the characters who will be most affected by the tragedy well before the murder takes place. In fiction as in poker, the higher the stakes, the bigger the payoff.

I'll use *What's Left Behind* to illustrate how spending time with the characters early in the novel pays dividends later. Joanne Kilbourn Shreve's son, Angus Kilbourn, discovers Lee Crawford's body on page 70, about one-fifth of the way into the novel. By this point, we have learned a number of facts about Lee that will become significant plot points later and produce provocative suspects.

Lee had a former lover against whom she recently had to take out a restraining order. When the order was issued, her ex had a breakdown and checked himself into a private psychiatric hospital. On the morning of the Crawford-Kilbourn wedding, he checked himself out of the facility. He spent five hours in a canoe on the lake watching in clear view of Lee and the others in front of the gazebo where the wedding was taking place. After the reception ended, the ex disappeared.

Lee's activism in support of the referendum that would put strict limits on the development of farmland has angered many, including a megadeveloper whose CEO has declared she will do whatever is necessary to stop Lee.

By taking the time to develop "secondary" characters, I was able to introduce several intriguing suspects with motives for murder. Equally significantly, readers have the chance to see Lee as a person of principle, determined to be a responsible steward of the land she inherited from her guardian, and as a warm, smart, generous, loving woman who shares a relationship with her twin that is life-enhancing for both.

Lee sparks intense emotions in people, and by the time she dies the reader is aware of the fact that to know her is not necessarily to love her. So in seventy pages I've dropped a number of hooks into the creek, and the reader has the rest of the book to see how the fishing expedition ends.

> *If a character isn't alive for you, he will never live for your readers.*—Margaret Maron, author of the Deborah Knott mystery series

BUILDING YOUR CHARACTERS

Prewrite. None of these little exercises will take much time at all, but they will give you a base for your character, and if you're lucky you will start to "hear" your character's voice.

1. Note what novelist Robertson Davies called "the police court facts" about your character: age, height, weight, colour of eyes, hair, and skin, distinguishing characteristics, place of birth, parents, siblings, education, occupation.
2. Do a Proustian questionnaire for each character. I've done a number of them for interviews, and they *are* revealing. The idea is that you're asked a question that's somewhat off-base and that you have to answer it without pausing to think. Some examples. "What's your biggest regret?" "What's your guilty pleasure?" "If you could be someone

in history, who would you be?" "Would you rather be able to travel through time or be invisible?" Your characters' answers to these unconventional questions might give you intriguing glimpses into their inner lives.

3. As a Virgo, I'm not a fan of stream-of-consciousness writing, but if you want to hear your character's voice this exercise is surprisingly effective.

In one of my early novels, I had a character who was a sociopath. I read a few articles about sociopaths, but nothing clicked, so I turned on my computer and started writing my character's autobiography. It didn't take long before I heard her voice. "My name is Maureen Gault. I was born on February 14th. My mama always said I was her little Valentine."

That was all I needed. When neighbours and teachers warned her mother that Maureen was doing some very bad things, her mother ignored them. After all, Maureen was "her little Valentine." And one day, when her mama was too busy looking out for her little Valentine to see the truth about her daughter, Maureen killed a man.

Not only did this exercise give me her voice, but also it explained the role her mother played in shaping Maureen into the person she became.

Discovering the formative experiences in your characters' lives will give you valuable material to work with. Sharing these experiences with your readers will lead them to deeper understandings of your characters' psyches.

4. Make sure each of your characters talks in a distinctive fashion. Choose diction that fits the character: too consciously cool, deliberately provocative, pug-

nacious, pompous, seductive, hypermasculine, butter wouldn't melt in her mouth, et cetera. Which actor would you choose to say that character's lines? For Maureen Gault, I chose the voice of the actress who played Heather Chandler, the meanest of the mean girls in the 1988 classic *Heathers*.

5. Give your character a particular haunt—a place that somehow defines her.
6. Allow your character to change in some fundamental way in the course of the novel. The change doesn't have to be as dramatic as Ebenezer Scrooge's 180 degree reversal on the meaning of Christmas, but revealing a glimmer of humanity in a seemingly unredeemable character will keep him from being a cutout figure. Conversely, showing a character flaw or a moment of weakness in an otherwise exemplary character will humanize him.

AVOIDING AUTHORIAL INTRUSION

Michael Connelly says "One telling detail will take you further than a page of description." Three examples: a character who can't pass a mirror without anxiously checking his or her reflection; an estranged parent who sends a child a birthday gift that reveals the parent has no knowledge of who his child really is; and a father who goes around to his dead son's friends at the gravesite thanking the young people for coming and apologizing for his broken English. Each of these telling details packs a real emotional wallop.

Let your reader come to know your characters the same way we come to know people in our lives: by their words, by their actions and reactions, by what they say and what others say about them. Give your readers the gift of getting to know your characters on their own.

> *The point of fiction is to give the reader for a few hours the chance to be somebody else, to broaden and deepen his understanding of himself and the strangers among whom he has to pass his days. The best novels do this now as they have always done it. It is a noble thing.*—Joseph Hansen, author of the Dave Brandstetter mystery series

RELIABLE SOURCES, SIDEKICKS, AND VILLAINS

A note to the reader: Joanne Kilbourn Shreve is hardly in the Holmes/Wolfe league, but as a writer you might find it helpful to see how a writer who is not Conan Doyle or Rex Stout struggles to put her own stamp on these conventions.

The repertory characters surrounding a sleuth who is not a member of the police force has a number of stalwarts. One is the *reliable source*, the person—perhaps a police officer, a private investigator, or a friendly journalist—who gives the protagonist access to inside information about cases.

When it comes to reliable sources, Nero Wolfe is blessed. In addition to the incomparable Archie Goodwin, Wolfe has a number of private detectives on whom he can rely. The most valued of them is Saul Panzer. The words Wolfe uses as he introduces Saul to a client show his regard for this PI, whose fees are robust but who is worth every penny. "That is Mr. Panzer, there at the end of Mr. Goodwin's desk," Wolfe says. "If he ever wants to know anything about you, tell him; you might as well." Wolfe and Inspector Cramer, head of the NYPD Homicide Division, have a grudging respect for one another. Cramer bristles at Wolfe's high-handedness, and Wolfe considers Cramer a plodder, but they collaborate on many cases.

In the Sherlock Holmes series, the Baker Street Irregulars are a group of street urchins led by an older boy, Wiggins, whom Holmes pays to collect data for his investigations. The rate is a shilling a day plus expenses with a one-guinea bonus for a vital clue. Holmes calls Inspector Tobias Gregson "the smartest of the Scotland Yarders," but because Holmes holds Scotland Yard detectives in low esteem this is faint praise. The two men work cooperatively on cases, and like Nero Wolfe and Inspector Kramer they regard each other coolly but with respect.

In my mystery series, the relationship between Debbie Haczkewicz and Joanne's husband, Zack Shreve, is both professional and personal. He is the mayor of Regina, and she is the chief of police, but they've known each other from the days when he was a trial lawyer and she was a police officer. Debbie likens their previous professional association to that between the orca and the great white shark, fierce natural enemies. The relationship changed when Debbie's teenage son, Leo, was in a motorcycle accident that left him a paraplegic. Determined to die, Leo lashed out at everyone who offered help. In desperation, Debbie went to Zack, and, after a month of often physical battles with Leo, Zack got through to him. Debbie characterizes her ongoing relationship with him this way: "Zack will always be a great white shark and I will always be an orca, but we've learned to cherish the times when we're able to swim side by side."

A first glance at the pantheon of mystery protagonists reveals that, more often than not, the sleuth has a *sidekick*. A second glance reveals that sleuth and sidekick are invariably polar opposites, but each has a skill or a quality that the other needs.

Exploring the relationships between the following sleuths and sidekicks will, I think, open up some possibilities for your own writing. Take a good look at the sleuth you have created. What skill or characteristic does he or she need that a sidekick might offer?

A Sherlockian friend sent me the following post she found online. She thought I would be interested, and I am. The question online was this: "In the relationship between Holmes and Watson who has the greatest need for the other?" Here are the question and the answer that intrigued my friend:

> Where would Holmes have been without his biographer and sounding board? Sherlock comments in *The Hounds of Baskerville* something to the effect that "some people see the light, others are conductors of the light and you John—you are a conductor." Watson was an integral part of Holmes' thought process, and he also acted as a counter balance, softening out the hard edges at the perimeter of Holmes' complex personality. Without Watson, I argue that Holmes would have been incomplete.

Nero Wolfe famously loathes working, and the idea of stepping out of his comfortable brownstone on West 35th Street is anathema to him. "I rarely leave my house," he says. "I do like it here. I would be an idiot to leave this chair, made to fit me." The Wolfe household is expensive to run, and when the household coffers are empty Archie Goodwin has to nag Wolfe to get back to work.

Wolfe is a man of thought. Goodwin, who narrates the stories, is a man of action. When they work together on cases, Nero does the thinking, and Archie is the legman. Again we see that opposites attract. As Nero introduces Archie to a client, we see again how the principal sleuth and the trusted assistant complete each other: "This is Mr. Goodwin, my confidential assistant. Whatever opinion you have formed of me includes him of necessity. His discretion is the twin of his valor."

> *The meeting of two personalities is like the contact of two chemical substances: if there is any reaction, both are transformed.*—Carl Jung

Readers are very protective of Joanne Kilbourn Shreve, and when in *The Last Good Day* she meets, falls in love with, and marries paraplegic, hard-driving, hard-living, trial lawyer Zack Shreve after knowing him for only five months I received a great deal of mail. Not much of it was congratulatory.

However, I had a sense that, as a couple, Joanne and Zack would be good for the series and good for each other. They have proven to be both. Zack is forty-eight and Joanne fifty-two when they fall in love. His doctor and poker partner tells Joanne that he's glad she's come along because Zack has been living like an eighteen year old with a death wish and that, if he keeps living at that frenetic pace, that death wish would come true.

The Last Good Day is the tenth book in the series, and I knew that both the series and Joanne needed the narrative possibilities that introducing her to the winner-take-all world of trial law would bring. I also suspected that readers would be interested in watching Zack, a man whose previous relationships with women seldom made it to breakfast, adjust to the realities of life with a wife and family.

Judging by my mail, Zack's conversion to doting family man has brought readers almost as much pleasure as it has brought me. Joanne and Zack are deeply in love. Their marriage is not an easy one, but it's a good one because, like the best of protagonists and sidekicks, they complete and transform each other.

In her 2002 book *Evil in Modern Thought*, Susan Neiman does not define what evil *is*; instead, she focuses on the effect evil *has*. Calling something evil, she writes, "is a way of marking the fact that it shatters our trust in the world. Evil is both harmful and inexplicable, but not just that; what defines an evil act is that it is permanently disorienting for all those touched by it." When it comes to creating your fictional *villain*, remember Neiman's explanation. As writers, it's important never to lose sight of the spoor an evil act leaves behind it.

James Lee Burke suggests "Crime fiction has come to replace the sociological novel of the 1930s and 1940s. It's a way of talking not only about the underside of America, what Michael Harrington called 'the Other America,' [but] it's a way of talking about larger society as well." Burke also notes:

> You meet only two or three kinds of villains in [my] stories and novels. You

> meet the run-of-the-mill miscreants, the people who get into trouble, but are still like the rest of us. Then you meet the second group, sociopaths. They are in the minority. The third group, the ones that Dave Robicheaux and Billy Bob Holland have the most trouble with, [are] those who have insinuated themselves into the mainstream of society. They're not legally criminals, but they do far more damage than people like Buchalter.

There are three distinct perspectives on evil. Understanding them will help you to identify the kind of villain that will best embody what you want to say about the presence of evil in the world.

First, evil is inherent in all human beings; in other words, it is a character problem. George Bernard Shaw used to say that some unfortunates are born without a thumb, whereas others are born without a moral sense. This perception that evil is inherent in all human beings suggests that evildoers are not monsters but ordinary people who, because of circumstances, are guilty, for a time at least, of monstrous behaviour. The old cartoon, *Pogo*, said it best: "We have met the enemy, and he is us."

Second, evil is a social problem, created by institutions that diminish or destroy the poor, the alienated, and the powerless. Much American crime fiction in the late twentieth century and early twenty-first century has been driven by the premise that, in an unjust and deeply flawed society in which humans and institutions are untrustworthy, individuals can combat evil only by trusting their instincts and remaining vigilant.

Third, evil is both inherent in who we are and susceptible to growth in a society whose citizens don't take their moral obligations to one another seriously. This belief is central to the work of many Canadian crime writers, including me.

And now, with a twirl of the Snidely Whiplash moustache, the villains!

As a writer, I loved hearing that Conan Doyle introduced the brilliant mathematician, crime lord Professor James Moriarty, as a device to get rid of Sherlock Holmes (of whom Conan Doyle was tiring). Readers rebelled. So, while Holmes was forced to flee across continental Europe to escape Moriarty's retribution, and while the pursuit did end on top of the Reichenbach Falls, where both Holmes and Moriarty appeared to fall to their deaths, appearance was not reality. The readers triumphed. Holmes lived on.

Crime lord Arnold Zeck is Nero Wolfe's Moriarty. He appears in only three Wolfe novels, but his relationship with Wolfe is riveting. Like Wolfe, Zeck is mysterious, brilliant, and arrogant. He's a formidable opponent for the man who occupies the specially built chair in the luxurious brownstone on West 35th Street, and Wolfe respects him. It's a battle of the titans, but in the novel *In the Best Families* Zeck goes too far. He intercepts a package of expensive sausages destined for Wolfe and puts tear gas in their place. The scale is tipped. Zeck must be defeated, and Wolfe takes drastic steps. He leaves the brownstone, puts it up for sale, and disappears until he has put the pieces for the end game in place.

Knowing your own darkness is the best method for dealing with the darknesses of other people.—Carl Jung

With the exception of three sociopaths, the murderers in the Joanne Kilbourn series are not monsters. They are ordinary people who find themselves in circumstances that, in their minds, justify the taking of a human life. Their very ordinariness often allows these murderers to slip beneath the radar, but Joanne's skill at detecting the darkness in others is finely honed. By nature a person given to rigorous self-examination, Joanne has come to understand the darkness in her own life. She is not quick to judge, but she is intuitive and logical, and when her intuition and logic suggest that someone could be guilty of murder she follows through.

In *12 Rose Street* and *What's Left Behind*, the villain is a megacorporation called Lancaster Development ruthlessly extracting everything it can from Regina and the farmland that surrounds it. When I was writing these two novels, Carl Hiassen's unforgettable gang of land rapists, crooked investors, corrupt politicians, dishonest developers, and garden-variety crooks was never far from my mind. His writing life has been devoted to protecting Florida, the state Hiassen loves. Although his villains are fictional, their real-life counterparts walk among us. Hiassen is never overtly didactic and always fun. If the villains in the novel you plan to write are like those mentioned above, then Hiassen is the writer to emulate. He has a light touch, but he can deliver a lethal uppercut when he needs to ensure that his bad guys are down for the count.

MINOR CHARACTERS

I love the tradition of Dickens, where even the most minor walk-on characters are twitching and particular and alive.—Donna Tartt

The difference between fiction that works and fiction that doesn't work can often be explained in two words: missed opportunities. In Middle English, some characters are known as "local characters" because their existence is limited to a particular place. The sole function of these characters is to deliver information or pick up a sword and then disappear from the narrative. Don't clutter your work with minor characters who simply pick up swords and walk away. Make your minor characters work for you.

First, engage your minor characters in a subplot. This can involve an on-again, off-again romance; efforts to derail the plans or the lives of the principal characters; or a mysterious figure who, like a figure in a Fellini movie, gains significance by appearing unexpectedly, then vanishing only to reappear, disappear, reappear, and disappear again.

In my novel *The Brutal Heart*, a street person never without her backpack filled with abandoned, dirty, and worn Care Bears repeatedly appears in the courthouse to yell threats at a client of Zack's law firm. The woman is dismissed because clearly she is a disturbed person off her meds, but in the end Joanne's sense that the woman has information that can bring a killer to justice leads to the novel's climax.

Subplots take the pressure off the central plot. They allow you to detour but keep the atmosphere tense without having to inject obviously contrived moments of suspense. If, at the end of your novel, the subplot can feed into a resolution of the central plot, then you've got yourself a winner.

Second, use minor characters to cool the emotional temperature. Murder is a dark subject, and your readers will need a respite from the tension and shadowy suspicions. Give your readers and your protagonists a breather by bringing in minor characters that lighten the mood while keeping the plot moving.

Third, minor characters can shed light on protagonists by revealing their histories, by acting as foils, or by showing a side of the protagonist that would otherwise not be evident. In *Gone Girl*, Gillian Flynn uses two minor characters to shed light on her protagonist, Nick. A search party has been organized to look for his missing wife, Amy. His quick sketch of one of the volunteers brings the woman to life and reveals his overheated libido: "She had an unnecessarily loud voice, a bit of a bray, like some enchanted, hot donkey." His description of a male character deftly reveals the man, but it also gives readers an insight into Nick's own psyche: "Desi seemed the definition of a gentleman: a guy who could quote a great poet, order a rare Scotch and buy a woman that right piece of vintage jewelry. . . . Across from him, I felt my suit wilt, my manners go clumsy. I had a swelling urge to discuss football and fart."

Fourth, minor characters can illuminate your theme. In *12 Rose Street*, the need for Joanne to forgive the friend who betrayed her illustrates the novel's theme that the only thing harder than forgiving is not forgiving.

Remember that every human being is the hero of his or her own story. Give your minor characters their day in the sun.

CHAPTER 8

PLOT

The plot is just a bribe to keep them reading.—
Kurt Vonnegut

In the glossary to his excellent text *Three Genres: The Writing of Poetry, Fiction, and Drama*, Stephen Minot offers the following definition of plot:

> The sequence of events, often divided into scenes in Fiction. It may be chronological, or it may be non-chronological in any of four ways: by *flashback* (inserting an earlier scene), by *multiple flashbacks*, by a *flash-forward* (rare) or by using a *frame* (beginning and ending the story or novel with the same scene).
>
> *Base time* refers to the primary plot from which flashbacks and, less often, flash-forwards depart. A *sub-plot* is a secondary plot that echoes or amplifies the main plot or provides *comic relief*.

> In traditional tragedies, the increasing complications are called *rising action*, the turning point is the *climax*, followed by *falling action*, which in turn leads to the *denouement*.

A few years ago CBC Radio invited me to write a five-minute mystery for its summer programming. All of the elements of plotting for a mystery are present in the 640 words of the short story CBC broadcast. Please consider "Eldorado" "a bribe to keep [you] reading" while illustrating the basics of plotting.

ELDORADO

Exposition: (Scene 1–The Opening) The night Cole Elliot moved into Precious Memories I was standing in the shadows with my walker, smoking the single cigarette I allow myself each day. From the first I knew that Cole did not belong in an extended care home. Most of our residents hadn't driven in years, but Cole arrived in a sleek, 1959 Cadillac Eldorado with tailfins that glowed in the moonlight. Cole glowed too. His snowy hair was thick; his tan was deep, and his teeth were improbably white. His step still had the spring of youth, and he carried his bags into the reception area unassisted.

(Scene 2)–Rising Action The next morning he arrived at breakfast wearing a periwinkle blue shirt that matched his eyes. *(The Catalyst) By the time the dishes were cleared, Cole had explained his presence*

to everyone's satisfaction but mine. His story was simple. He was a widower who missed his wife's companionship and her cooking, so he moved into Precious Memories. I was not convinced. Intellectually, most of us had long since passed our best-before date, and the meals were a succession of grayish-brown casseroles and dishes with names like Hawaiian Surprise.

(Scene 3) I watched as Cole attached himself to Angel, the frail blonde across the hall from me. The first time I met Angel, she told me she'd been at Woodstock, then in a sweet voice she sang the Joni Mitchell song about the weekend that changed history. The next time I saw Angel, she repeated her performance note for note. Every afternoon, as Cole helped her into the passenger seat of *his* Eldorado, Angel was warbling "Woodstock." Cole was singing a different song. Once, as I passed them in the hall, I overheard him urging Angel to give him power of attorney.

(Scene 4) Death is a fact of life at Precious Memories, and when Angel unexpectedly made her way back to the garden I felt a pang. Cole did not. At dinner that night, he sat with Rita Dolcetti, an ex-showgirl who had married well. The next day Rita took Angel's place beside Cole in the Eldorado. Ten days later Rita, like Angel, passed away in her sleep.

(Scene 5) That night when I went out for my smoke, I witnessed an odd tableau.

Cole approached his Cadillac, stroked her flaring fins, inserted his key into her trunk, removed a lockbox, and filled it with cash. *(The catalyst pushes the action toward the climax)* Logic suggested that Cole was paving the way to his own city of gold with the assets of the women of Precious Memories, but I needed proof.

(Scene 6) The next morning, when I dithered about needing help with my investments, Cole had me in the passenger seat of his Eldorado headed for my bank within the hour.

My investment portfolio was robust; nonetheless, Cole was concerned. He suspected I was anemic and recommended a vitamin regimen. As a retired pharmacist, I immediately recognized Cole's "vitamins" as depressants that, in combination with other drugs, could kill.

Climax: (Scene 7) Steeling myself for the task ahead took time, but on a balmy June night I brought along my BlackBerry to photograph Cole counting his cash. I had him nicely lined up when a cat leapt out of the bushes, straight into my walker. As the cat yowled, Cole looked at me with distaste. "I never trusted you," he said. "Secret smokers have no moral centre."

I moved my walker toward his car. "It's your word against mine," he said, slamming the trunk. Cigarette between my lips, I removed the cap on the gas tank. Cole was too quick for me. My intention

> had been to blow up the Cadillac, but just as I threw my lit cigarette toward the gas tank Cole jumped into the front seat.
>
> *Denouement: (Scene 8)* The lockbox with the cash was fireproof. Cole was not. His memorial service was held at Precious Memories. We buried Cole with the ashes of his Eldorado.

Most mystery novels have a word count of somewhere between 80,000 and 100,000 words, so the "rules" here are just a guide. That said, they do work for novels too.

OPENING

Don't ramble. You'll lose your reader. Move quickly into the mind of the character who is your reader's means of perceiving the story. Details about setting and character can be added later. Note how the salient details about menu and inhabitants at Precious Memories are inserted into the exposition. Note also that the details do not overshadow the effectiveness of the opening.

John Irving, author of *A Prayer for Owen Meany*, believes that the *opening* sentence should contain the entire novel. The opening sentence of that book is lengthy, and Irving does need a semicolon to help with the heavy lifting, but the entire novel is there: "I am doomed to remember a boy with a wrecked voice—not because of his voice, or because he was the smallest person I ever knew, or even because he was the instrument of my mother's death, but because he is the reason I believe in God; I am a Christian because of Owen Meany." Most of us aren't in Irving's league, but the point is clear. Don't waste your first sentence or your first paragraph. Cut to the chase.

The *catalyst* is the plot point that precipitates the action. When our unnamed narrator's suspicions about Cole Elliot are alerted ("By the time the dishes were cleared, Cole had explained his presence to everyone's satisfaction but mine"), the action begins.

RISING ACTION

From that point on, the narrator-protagonist is watching and assessing Cole. She is looking for proof that he is up to no good, and proof is not long in coming. Cole selects and zooms in on Angel, a particularly vulnerable resident of Precious Memories. After the narrator overhears Cole asking Angel to give him power of attorney, the tension rises. When, after her death, he begins to repeat his modus operandi on Rita Dolcetti, another resident of Precious Memories, and she, too, dies, the protagonist knows she must get the proof she needs to stop him. From the moment the narrator decides to use herself as bait to catch the killer, the reader is hooked.

PACING

Pacing the plot of a 640-word story is easy; pacing the plot of an 80,000–100,000-word manuscript is not. But here are some strategies that should help you to pace your plot.

Follow the Goldilocks rule by avoiding extremes. Mysteries are about revealing what has been concealed. Make sure the rate at which you reveal your plot points is neither too fast, nor too slow, but just right. Don't keep the action moving so rapidly that your readers feel as if they're standing on the receiving end of a fire hose, and don't submerge your readers in a molasses swamp of unnecessary reflections, descriptions, and so on.

Aim for Aristotle's "golden mean." Find the perfect balance between action and reflection. Consider alternating passages of rapid-fire plot development with more leisurely passages of description or contemplation. Stephen Minot has a useful metaphor: "[An ideal] pace of fiction often resembles the technique of an experienced skater: The forward thrust is followed by a glide." To extend his metaphor, if a skater's performance is all forward thrusts, then there is movement but no grace. If the skater focuses primarily on glides, then her performance might have beauty but will lack energy and momentum. Writers, take note!

Wait until you have a complete first draft to review the pacing of your novel. As you read the draft, the problem areas will quickly become apparent. A section where there are too many "thrusts" will have the hiccup breathlessness of a child describing a movie ("and then . . . and then . . . and then . . . "). A section where there are too many "glides" will lack vigour and slow the momentum.

The strategy for correcting both problems is the same. Ask yourself, "What do I hope to achieve with this piece of writing? What is my theme? What do I want to say about living a life?" If your manuscript is so action driven that it seems to lack thought or heart, then try inserting a scene or two in which the protagonist reflects on the meanings and possible consequences of what's happened or speculates about why the characters involved in a particular incident felt compelled to act as they did. While the character is speculating, give him or her something interesting to do—planting a garden, putting up Christmas lights, making chicken soup—something that will humanize your character and retain your reader's interest.

Man Booker Prize winner Hilary Mantel suggests concentrating your narrative energy on the point of change: "When your character is new to a place or things alter around them, that's the point to step back and fill in the details of their world." I would add that the point of change is also the logical place for your character to reflect on the effects of recent events on her life and speculate about what will happen next. This tactic will slow the rate of revelation but keep the reader's interest high.

There is no Cialis that will cause a flaccid manuscript to suddenly pulse with life, but there are some solutions. If you're still working with a first draft, consider introducing a subplot. Think about your protagonist's domestic life. Police officers, lawyers, and disillusioned private eyes have been known to fall in love with people who, for one reason or another, spell trouble. A subplot in which a protagonist is powerfully attracted to a person who plays a significant role in the story, fights a prolonged battle against the attraction, and then agonizes over how to resolve the relationship once and for all will bring energy to your manuscript and add depth to your characterization of the protagonist.

Carl Jung (there he is again!) says we are drawn to people who complete us. What can an ill-starred romance reveal to the protagonist about herself? What can it reveal about her to your readers? If there's a spouse in the picture, for whom will the reader be rooting? What, ultimately, does the protagonist decide to do? How does her decision affect the outcome of the action? A subplot takes the pressure off your main plot, creates interest in your protagonist's inner life, gives you a new and intriguing character to work with, and creates suspense.

The red herring, a clue or character intended to be misleading, has long been a staple of the mystery genre. If the red herring is a character, then he or she must be a logical choice for the culprit. Although ultimately the protagonist will discover that the red herring is innocent, the pursuit of a false lead can add some zing to your limping narrative. Remember, it's not the destination that counts; it's the journey.

SCENE

In fiction, a *scene* is a unit of action marked either by a shift in the number of characters or by a shift in time and place. The keywords in this definition are *unit of action* and *shift*.

In conversation, we make this division all the time. Without thinking, we subordinate unimportant units of action to quickly bring focus to the significant episode we want to discuss. For example, if you ran into me in the hall at the university on the first day of classes and saw I was agitated, you'd ask me if there was something wrong. In answering you, I would subordinate a couple of minor irritations (out of coffee at home, stuck in traffic on my way to work) to get to the source of my frustration and anger. A computer glitch had scheduled ninety students in my English 100 class, which should have been limited to thirty students and which had been allotted a classroom that accommodated thirty students. Not surprisingly, when I walked into the room, the students, all on the first day of their first semester, were confused and upset. It took me the rest of the morning dealing with boneheads to straighten out the situation. I'd end my account with a summing up: "Anyway, crisis over; the registrar's office is dealing with it, so I'm not going to throw myself under a bus." A scene must involve a shift of some kind—either physical or mental. That particular scene involves a mental shift from problem to solution, from annoyance to relief.

Sometimes, as in Scene 6 of "Eldorado," the shift is both physical and mental. Physically, the protagonist sets herself up as bait; Cole takes the bait, and they drive in his Eldorado to her bank. Satisfying himself that her portfolio is healthy, he prescribes a regimen of "vitamins" that our narrator, a retired pharmacist, recognizes as medication that could kill her. But the significant shift for the narrator is mental: she moves from well-founded suspicion to concrete proof. The scene, having done its work, ends.

You don't have to mark every scene in your 80,000–100,000-word novel, but remember that every scene in a well-wrought novel has a purpose. Reviewing your first draft is an ideal time to isolate scenes that aren't carrying their weight. Make those scenes more effective by adding material that makes them somehow advance the purpose of the novel or by combining them with other scenes. If neither option works, then ditch the scene altogether.

PLOT AND STRUCTURE

Plot is what happens. *Structure* is the order in which what happens is presented. The events in most novels are presented in chronological order: that is, they follow a generally linear timeline from the beginning of the story to its conclusion.

Nonlinear narrative, disjointed narrative, or disrupted narrative presents events out of chronological order to suit the writer's purpose. These techniques are frequently used in movies, where they can be integrated into the main story with relative ease. Writers of fiction dealing with parallel plotlines or a story narrated within the main plotline might find these methods congenial.

Technically, a *flashback* must be an entire scene (setting and dialogue included) that takes place before the base time of the plot. I'm going to stretch the definition to include those flashes of memory we all experience that seemingly come out of nowhere but have powerful impacts on our emotions or perceptions.

In fiction as in life, a flashback can be ignited by a scent, a piece of music, a shaft of light, or, in Proust's case, a madeleine. I don't believe I've ever written an entire scene as a flashback, but because I use a first-person narrator I find brief but intense bursts of memory (mini flashbacks?) useful tools for conveying Joanne's emotions and insights.

Angus Kilbourn bears a startling resemblance to his late father, Ian. After Joanne learns about Ian's affair, Angus's gesture of running his fingers through his hair to tame a wayward lock–a gesture startlingly like his father's–stabs Joanne with memories of both her deep love for her former husband and his betrayal. A major theme of *12 Rose Street* is betrayal and forgiveness, and these mini flashbacks allowed me to show how fraught her path to forgiveness is.

Agatha Christie's genteel spinster sleuth Miss Marple is frequently able to solve crimes because of flashbacks that conjure up memories of nasty behaviour in her sleepy village of St. Mary Mead. These flashbacks to incidents that, in some way, parallel the crime that Miss Marple is currently confronting have a way of leading Christie's disarmingly chatty sleuth to the truth about the identity and motivation of the murderer.

Christie's use of flashbacks to solve crimes works because Miss Marple is such a perfectly realized character. We know that she is a shrewd observer of human nature and that her keen intelligence will lead her to bring what she has seen in the past to understand the present. Readers accept her method of solving crimes without question because of what they know about the character.

The Miss Marple novels demonstrate that, in the right hands, flashbacks can be a handy tool for the writer of crime fiction. By all means, make use of them, but be sparing. Make sure the flashback always advances the story, and don't let it overshadow the baseline of your narrative. Remember Stephen King's sage advice: "Don't let the tail wag the dog."

A *flash-forward* is rare in part, I think, because, in giving the reader information the characters don't have, it puts distance between reader and character that lessens the emotional impact of a piece. With great trepidation, I began *The Winners Circle* (2017) with a half-page flash-forward. I was uneasy about it, but my editor and I agreed that my reason for taking the plunge was sound. The murders don't take place till page 230, near the end of the book. I wanted readers to know and care about the doomed characters and their situations before the tragedy occurs, so the novel opens with a flash-forward to Joanne reflecting on her state of mind in the weeks following the unbearable losses.

So far there have been no complaints, so it appears the strategy worked.

ENDING

Near the top of the list of words I've taken a solemn oath never to use is *closure*. Yet closure, the sense that the story you have been telling is fully completed, is one of the goals you must achieve before you pat yourself on the back for crossing the finish line.

If your readers don't feel that click of closure when they reach the end of your novel, then they will be dissatisfied. Instead of contemplating the pleasant prospect of mentally revisiting your characters' ideas and adventures, they'll be reaching for their pitchforks and asking, "What the heck happened?"

The HBO series *The Sopranos* offers definitive proof of the case for closure. Nearly 12 million people watched "Made in America," the eighty-sixth and final episode of the series. For over six years, viewers had been avidly involved in the lives of crime boss Tony Soprano and his extended family. The writing for the series was superb, and the plot lines leading up to the finale promised a stunning ending.

Stunning it was. Tony, his wife Carmella, their daughter Meadow, and their son A. J. meet in a restaurant favoured by mob members for a family meal. Tony's position with the mob has become increasingly precarious, and every viewer expects at least one member of the family to get whacked before the credits roll. And then ten seconds before the episode ends, while the Soprano family chats and scans the menus under the watchful eyes of several other restaurant customers, including a chillingly menacing man in a "Members Only" jacket, the screen fades to black and stays black until the final credits roll.

At that point, to paraphrase Yeats, mere anarchy was loosed upon the land. At approximately 9:55 P.M. on June 10, 2007, nearly 12 million people throughout North America picked up their remotes and threw them at their TV screens. They had been cheated of closure, and they weren't going to take it. An online search for "last episode of the Sopranos" reveals that, after over a decade, those ten seconds of black screen still rankle viewers.

Lesson 1 about ending your novel is clear: give your readers closure.

Lesson 2 is at the heart of the covenant between writers of crime fiction and their readers: tie up all loose ends—no exceptions, no excuses.

Lesson 3: give your readers their second "aha" moment by revealing a truth that allows them to see the experience of being human in a new light. Note the word *reveal.* This is where you, as a writer, must take a giant step back and remember that good writing always shows rather than tells.

Your ending doesn't need to be dramatic; in fact, it can be very simple—a small gesture, an exchange of words, a glimpse of something that suddenly assumes significance because everything in the novel has pointed toward the insight it brings. This is the moment for your reader (and perhaps your protagonist) to experience an epiphany.

Epiphany is a word that originally recognized a Christian festival held on January 6 in honour of the three wise men who saw a star in the east and, believing that it signalled a change in the world, journeyed to see the infant Jesus Christ. The stories in James Joyce's collection *The Dubliners* centre on the idea of an epiphany, the moment when something occurs that suddenly makes us see and understand life in a new and clear way. Look at the endings of those five novels you examined earlier. Any epiphanies there?

Some critics see an epiphany in the contentious ten seconds of black screen that end *The Sopranos*. In the July 29, 2015, edition of the blog *Observer Culture*, Vinnie Mancuso's article "Ten Seconds of Black: Revisiting the Life-Affirming Series Finale of *The Sopranos*" argues convincingly that writer David Chase's ending for the last episode was inspired:

> David Chase took it to the extreme and literally left us in the dark, and it was the finest thing he could have done. I never understood why the lingering question is always "Does Tony die?" Because *of course* he dies, eventually. So does AJ. So does Carmella. So does the man in the Members Only jacket, along with everyone else in that diner. And then the world will go on without them. Tony's life, whether it lasts another ten seconds or fifty years, will go on until it doesn't.
>
> There just won't be an audience around to watch anymore.
>
> Those ten seconds of black represent not only the rest of Tony's life, but the rest of our own. It is at the same time the most frustrating and the most comforting series finale of all time. It abruptly cuts to a blank screen, but there was an entire

> life lived before that blank screen, and there will be life after it no matter how short. Life goes on until the end credits.

Now *that's* an epiphany!

CHAPTER 9
STYLE

Write in a way that comes naturally.
–Strunk and White

If it sounds like writing, I rewrite it.
–Elmore Leonard

In his glossary to *Three Genres*, Stephen Minot gives a concise and useful definition of *style* as "The manner in which a work is written. It is determined by the author's decisions, both conscious and unconscious, regarding diction; syntax; narrative mode (relative importance of dialogue, thoughts, action, description) and pace (the reader's sense of progress). It is closely connected with tone, the emotion generated by the work itself."

The overall effect of the novel you write will be determined by the words you choose and how you put them on the page. This chapter addresses how you can ensure that, to paraphrase Samuel Coleridge, you put the best words in the best order to achieve what you set out to achieve with your novel.

Diction refers simply to the words you use. In life, much of what we know about people comes not simply from *what* they say but also from *how* they say it. The vocabulary you choose for your characters can reveal a great deal about who they are. Following are samples of dialogue from three characters in the Nero Wolfe novel *The Rubber Band* (1934). Note how in each case the diction complements the sentiment expressed.

The first speaker is Wolfe:

> It has been many years since any woman has slept under this roof. Not that I disapprove of them, except when they attempt to function as domestic animals. When they stick to the vocations for which they are best adapted, such as chicanery, sophistry, self-adornment, cajolery, mystification and incubation, they are sometimes splendid creatures.

The second speaker is Clara Fox, a client in residence, pouring Archie Goodwin's after-dinner coffee in the dining room while wearing his yellow dressing gown:

> You know, Mr. Goodwin, this house represents the most insolent denial of female rights the mind of man has ever conceived. No woman in it from top to bottom, but the routine is faultless, the food is perfect, and the sweeping and dusting are impeccable. I have never been a housewife, but I can't overlook this challenge. I'm going to marry Mr. Wolfe, and I know a girl that will be just the

> thing for you, and of course our friends will be in and out a good deal. This place needs some upsetting.

And the third speaker is Goodwin:

> I know pretty well what my field is. Aside from my primary function as the thorn in the seat of Wolfe's chair to keep him from going to sleep and waking up only for meals, I'm chiefly cut out for two things: to jump and grab something before the other guy can get his paws on it, and to collect pieces of the puzzle for Wolfe to work on.

Spoiler alert! Despite Clara's many charms, Wolfe does not revise his forcefully expressed opinion of women. He remains a bachelor, as does Goodwin.

When I read these passages, I can hear the voices of Nero, Clara, and Archie. Give each of your characters a distinctive way of speaking. The section on minor characters suggests strategies you can use to find your character's voice. Now is the time to bring those strategies into play.

Following are some considerations when you choose the words you're going to put in a character's mouth.

First, how old is the character? Child narrators are tricky. If you're considering using a young narrator, decide carefully on age. Children perceive things differently at different stages in their development, and for that reason they can be untrustworthy as narrators. (Remember that golden oldie "I Saw Mommy Kissing Santa Claus"?) Give the child a vocabulary that is believable and convincing. In *Room*, Emma Donoghue used Jack, a five-year-old narrator, affectingly. In *The Curious Incident of the Dog in the Night-Time*, Mark Haddon's narrator is Christopher Boone, a fifteen year old who describes himself as "a mathematician with some behavioural difficulties," and this choice of narrator works brilliantly. Jonathan Safran Foer's nine-year-old narrator-protagonist, Oskar Schell, who sets out on a quest when he discovers a key after his father is killed on 9/11, is a fully realized character who offers the reader a heartbreaking perspective on how a child deals with grief. These books are all mysteries worth reading, and they'll give you solid ideas about how to avoid missteps when you match vocabulary to a young character.

Second, how educated is the character? This question is not as elitist as it might sound. Facility with language can make a person soar, but it can also create barriers. Parents who have not had the advantage of a solid education can believe that an educated child suddenly thinks he or she is "too good" for the family. Educated children can be dismissive or ashamed of parents with less formal education.

Minot defines *dialect* as "dialogue that echoes a regional or ethnic speech pattern." He goes on to note that, "With some exceptions, it is achieved by word choice and word order rather than the obtrusive use of phonetic spelling." Using dialect in your writing is tricky. There is always the danger that it seems to demean your character.

In his novel *Creole Belle*, James Lee Burke, author of the Dave Robicheaux mystery series, has his protagonist, himself Creole, explain the patois:

> As with many Creoles and Cajuns, there was a peculiarity at work in Tee Jolie's speech. She was ungrammatical and her vocabulary was limited, but because of the cadence in her language and her regional accent, she was always pleasant to listen to, a voice from a gentler and more reserved time, even when what she spoke of was not pleasant to think about.

The following passage shows the melody of Tee Jolie's speech:

> "I always had my music and the piece of land my father left me and my sister and my mama," she said. "I sang wit' BonSoir, Catin. I was queen of the Crawfish Festival in Breaux Bridge. I t'ink back on that, and it's like it was ten years ago instead of two. A lot can change in a short time, cain't it? My mama died. Now it's just me and my li'l sister, Blue and my granddaddy back in St. Martinville."

Incidentally the *New York Times* calls Burke America's best novelist. Not America's best *mystery* novelist, but America's *best novelist*, period. If you haven't read him, you should. He does everything right.

Third, what does the speaker intend his or her words to convey? Most of us have different personae for different situations, and that means we use language differently depending on the situation. My diction when I deliver a lecture is different from the language I use with my young grandchildren and their friends.

For good or ill, we use words to communicate. Words can be tools, but they can also be weapons. Words can be used as shields to keep others from seeing perceived vulnerability or weakness.

Never forget the power of silence. Words not spoken and questions not answered can send a powerful message. Harold Pinter's use of long pauses and silence in *The Homecoming* shows how people use them to communicate in their daily lives. Think of the last time someone gave you "the silent treatment." The memory will be painful, but it will be a compelling reminder that Pinter's is a lesson worth learning.

When you're considering the best words to put on the page, remember American poet E. A. Robinson's observation: "Poetry tries to tell us something that cannot be said." The solution to bridging the gap between what you need to say and the limitations of the vernacular might be found in your old poetry notes from first-year English.

> *Don't tell me the moon is shining: show me the glint of light on broken glass.*—Anton Chekov

ABSTRACT VERSUS CONCRETE

Paint a picture. Make the abstract concrete. An exercise I liked to use with my English 100 students drives home this point. I asked them to close their eyes, and when I said a word they were to tell me the images that appeared in their minds. As the two columns below demonstrate, the associations my students made were instructive.

Abstract *Concrete*
brave ....firefighter
spicy................pizza
soothing ....massage
sexy..................my boy/girlfriend (smart answer!)
disgusting ....vomit

We cannot envision an abstraction. We will always respond to it with a concrete image, and that image will be something we can see, hear, touch, smell, or taste. Whenever possible, go for the concrete image in your writing. It is forceful, and it will connect with your reader.

Much of my novel *Kaleidoscope* is set in North Central Regina, an area that *Maclean's* characterized as "the worst neighbourhood in Canada." North Central is plagued by poverty, hopelessness, and their inevitable corollaries alcoholism, drug addiction, violence, and prostitution. Many of those selling their bodies are children not yet in their teens.

Seeing a child as young as one of my children and later as young as one of my grandchildren standing with dead eyes on street corners waiting to service an adult sickened me. Like many Reginans, I had read reports, signed petitions, and attended meetings about the abomination of child prostitution. But there were still children on street corners.

In *Kaleidoscope*, Joanne and her family have just moved into a condo in a renovated warehouse in the area. Joanne is out for an early morning run with a friend when there's an incident:

> When we turned onto Rose Street, a late-model black SUV peeled past us. The

> vehicle slowed but didn't stop at the stop sign on the corner. The door on the passenger side opened and someone threw a large bundle onto the pavement, slammed the door closed again, and the SUV sped off. The incident was over in a matter of seconds. . . . As we came closer to the corner, we heard crying: what had appeared to be discarded clothing was a naked Aboriginal child, perhaps nine years old, wrapped in a blanket. She was clutching a ten-dollar bill, and her eyes were wide with terror. A grey-white viscous substance was dribbling from her mouth.

The viscous substance is semen.

I did scores of readings after *Kaleidoscope* was published, and invariably someone in the audience would bring up that scene. Often they would be angry with me for writing about something they deemed disgusting. I would agree that the image is disgusting, but, when I pointed out that the child represented scores of children forced into prostitution on our city's streets, we were able to discuss the real problem. One concrete image can leave an indelible impression in your reader's mind. Strong nouns, verbs, and images can help readers to see what you want them to see.

SYNTAX

Syntax means sentence structure, and as always the rule is to make certain the length and complexity of the sentences you write serve the novel. Trust your ear. Read several pages aloud. An unremitting barrage of short sentences will move the pace along but can make your writing seem choppy. Long sentences slow the pace, but they can also put your reader to sleep, so *generally* the Goldilocks rule applies: not too many short sentences, not too many long sentences. Find the right balance.

NARRATIVE MODE

The *exposition* gives readers information about the novel, where they are, and whom they are with. In the opening of his novel *Lush Life*, Richard Price does it all in a single sentence (John Irving would be pleased): "The Quality of Life Task Force: four sweatshirts in a bogus taxi set up on the corner of Clinton Street alongside the Williamsburg Bridge off-ramp to profile the incoming salmon run; their mantra: Dope, guns, overtime; their motto: Everyone's got something to lose."

In the next passage, the reader meets the four cops who, like many members of the NYPD, will be among the novel's major characters. The reader learns their thoughts, sees them in action, and becomes familiarized with the setting of the action. The reader is now firmly in the world of *Lush Life*.

> Lugo, Daley, Geohagan, Scharf [. . .] all in their thirties, which, at this late hour, made them some of the oldest white men on the Lower East Side.
>
> Forty minutes without a nibble . . .
>
> Restless, they finally pull out to honeycomb the narrow streets for an hour of

> endless tight right turns: falafel joint, jazz joint, gyro joint, corner. Schoolyard, crêperie, realtor, corner. Tenement, tenement, tenement museum, corner.

As Price goes on for another eight similar, repetitive sentences to list without comment or description the buildings the four officers pass as they make endless "tight right turns" honeycombing the area, readers see what the officers see and feel their boredom and growing frustration. After an hour, the four cops are itching for action, and they spot a possibility. Driven by their mantra and their motto, they move in.

> Daley and Lugo slowly walk up on either side of the car, cross-beam the front seats. The driver, a young green-eyed Latino, rolls down his window. "Officer, what I do?"
>
> Lugo rests his crossed arms on the open window as if it's a backyard fence. "License and registration, please?"
>
> [. . .]
>
> Passing over his papers. "All serious, Officer, and no disrespect intended, maybe I can learn something here, but what did I do?"
>
> "Primary, you have neon trim on your plates."
>
> "Hey, I didn't put it there. This my sister's whip."
>
> "Secondary, your windows are too dark."
>
> "I *told* her about that."
>
> "Tertiary, you crossed a solid yellow."
>
> "To get around a double-parked car."

> "Quadrary, you're sitting by a hydrant."
> "That's 'cause you just pulled me over."
> Lugo takes a moment to assess the level of mouth he's getting.
> As a rule he is soft-spoken, leaning in to the driver's window to conversate, to explain, his expression baggy with patience, going eye to eye as if to make sure what he's explicating here is being digested, seemingly deaf to the obligatory sputtering [. . .] of verbal abuse, but . . . if the driver says that one thing, goes one word over some invisible line, then without any change of expression, without any warning signs except maybe a slow straightening up, a sad/disgusted looking off, he steps back, reaches for the door handle, and the world as they knew it, is no more.

Price mixes action, dialogue, and exposition to bring the character of Lugo to life. Notice Lugo's diction ("primary, secondary, tertiary, quadrary"), his patience in making certain his words are being understood, and his willingness to ignore verbal abuse. Lugo is a by-the-book cop until a suspect "goes one word over some invisible line."

In five pages, Price has established the novel's *tone*. The novel deals with inherently powerful material and emotions, but Price allows his material to speak for itself. *Lush Life* is filled with skilful writing, but none of it is ornate or heightened.

In the 1950s, there was a TV show about the LAPD called *Dragnet*. The hero was Sergeant Joe Friday; he was all business, and if a witness (usually female) was embellishing her story he would say, in a monotone, "Just the facts, ma'am. Just the facts."

From the outset of *Lush Life*, Price is in command of his material. He gives readers everything they need to know about the crime and the investigation without embellishment or authorial intrusion. Like the four officers of The Quality of Life Task Force and the score of other police officers in the novel, the reader hears the voices and sees the faces of victims, bystanders, witnesses, the bereaved, and the murderer. Readers have "the facts," and sometimes the facts are heartbreaking. In the following passage, a father has just identified the body of his murdered son in the police morgue. Note the small but telling detail of "the acoustically tiled walls" specifically designed to swallow grief.

> Marcus stood up, shook the detective's hand, straightened his shirt and took a step to the door, then wheeled back around and let loose with a single whooping sob that should have been heard all through the building but was swallowed by the acoustically tiled walls: specifically installed, Iacone had once been told, in anticipation of moments such as this.

Minot's glossary defines *pace* as reflecting the readers' "sense that a story . . . moves rapidly or drags. This is determined by the rate of revelation and the style." The pace of *Lush Life* mirrors the pace of the investigation: mind-numbingly slow as the officers encounter dead end upon dead end, heart-stopping in the face of human pain, and pulse-quickening as the facts come together and the truth is revealed.

The rule about style is that the techniques a writer uses should not be noticeable. All that matters is the end result, the novel your readers are holding. Readers don't want to know how the magician saws the lady in half; they simply want to marvel at the fact he can.

CHAPTER 10

CREATING A ROBUST SERIES

I always enjoy Q&A sessions because they give me a chance to learn what's in readers' minds. Some of the questions surprise me. One library patron wondered if I'd brought Joanne Kilbourn's brisket recipe with me to the reading. (I hadn't, but I did email the recipe to her when I got back to the hotel.) Brisket aside, three questions always seem to crop up. How long do I plan to continue writing the series? What factors contribute to the longevity of a series? And how do I plan to end the series?

I've known the answer to the first question for a while. From the beginning, the character of Joanne Kilbourn Shreve has been a gift to me as a writer and as a person. Every time I open my laptop the prospect of creating Joanne, her family, her friends, and her life brings me joy. Going on set in Toronto to watch six of my set-in-Saskatchewan novels being magically transformed into made-for-TV movies and travelling across Canada more times than I can count to attend writers' festivals, where I'm spoiled and have a chance to sit down and talk books with readers and other writers who become friends, have enriched my life immeasurably. Joanne has opened doors to many new worlds for me. I owe her far too much to continue writing the series when it becomes a job rather than a blessing. So the answer to the first question is that the series will end when I can no longer bring my best self to it. I don't know when that will happen, so I have no answer for the third question.

I can take a stab, however, at answering the second question. Those of you reading this book because you're planning to start your first mystery novel might think that talking about long-term success has no relevance for you, but since 1988, when I began writing *Deadly Appearances*, I've stumbled onto some useful truths about strategies that can contribute to a lengthy and robust life for your planned series. I'll start at the beginning.

In his 2004 book *The Seven Basic Plots: Why We Tell Stories*, Christopher Booker identifies seven basic plots:

1. Overcoming the monster (*Beowulf*, *Jaws*)
2. Rags to riches (*Aladdin*, *Oliver Twist*)
3. The quest (*Odyssey*, *Watership Down*)
4. Comedy (Aristophanes, Marx Brothers)
5. Tragedy (*Oedipus*, *Macbeth*)
6. Rebirth (*Sleeping Beauty*, *A Christmas Carol*)
7. Voyage and return (*Peter Rabbit*, *Brideshead Revisited*)

The plot lines driven by Booker's list of possibilities will vary dramatically, as will the stories they produce. But whether you choose to write a rags-to-riches story, an account of a quest, an exploration of a rebirth, or a tale of voyage and return, your protagonist will encounter many characters, and each will play a specific role in developing your story's plot. That said, the function of these characters goes well beyond pushing the story line forward.

Booker makes a significant point:

> However many characters may appear in a story, its real concern is with just one: its hero or heroine. It is he with whose fate we identify, as we see him gradually developing towards that state of self-realization which marks the end of the story. Ultimately it is in relation to this central figure that all other characters in a story take on their significance. What each of the other characters represents is really only some aspect of the inner state of the hero or heroine themselves.

Amen!

If, heaven forfend, I were forced to write a master's thesis on my novels, I would title it "Gail Bowen's Joanne Kilbourn Novels: An Ordinary Woman's Journey to Self-Realization and the Beginning of Wisdom." That snore-inducing title would not land me a lucrative job in my publisher's sales and marketing division, but as a writer who reads and answers every piece of mail I receive I know that readers come to my books because Joanne is someone with whom they would like to have coffee. They want to know what's happening in her life, and they want to know how what is happening is affecting her.

STRATEGY 1

I'm going to begin by discussing a handful of characters who have a profound effect on Joanne's growing understanding and acceptance of the woman she is. I'm not a literary theorist, but as I said I have–more by good luck than by good planning–come up with a couple of strategies that will get your series off to a strong start and allow it to flourish. This tactic will require some serious thought at the beginning, but it will pay regular and rewarding dividends. Here is the first strategy: *as early as possible, introduce some secondary characters who have intriguing back stories of their own and whose connections with your protagonist will endure and evolve throughout your novels.*

Howard Dowhanuik is introduced on the second page of my first novel, *Deadly Appearances*. Writing the beginning of a novel is difficult. Writing the beginning of a first novel is straight-out terrifying. The writer must introduce the reader to the world of the novel and its characters. Because I use a first-person narrator/protagonist, I had to give readers enough information about Joanne's past and present to engage them and convince them to trust Joanne as the narrator.

In other words, I had to ease a substantial amount of expository material into the narrative. The word *exposition* comes from Latin, and its literal meaning is "a showing forth." You "show forth" enough background information to allow your readers to make sense of the story you are about to tell. Finding a balance between too many facts and too few facts is tough, but as you navigate that narrow channel remember the cardinal rule of writing: show, don't tell.

On page 2 of *Deadly Appearances*, Joanne tells us that Howard had been the premier of her province for eleven years, the leader of the official opposition for seven years, and her friend for all that time and more. The time is the present, but the setting is an old-fashioned political picnic with softball games, a chicken barbecue, a fiddler, and of course speeches. The purpose of the picnic is to celebrate the victory of Andy Boychuk, the new leader of Joanne and Howard's political party, and to salve the wounds of the men and women he defeated in the nomination race. By page 11, Andy has been murdered, but we have learned enough from the casual conversation of long-time friends Howard and Joanne to know where we are, the nature of their relationship, who the people around them are, and who might have wanted Andy dead.

Initially Howard is a tool with which I introduced expository material unobtrusively. Later in *Deadly Appearances* he helps readers to understand the dynamics among the men and women in Andy's life. Perhaps more importantly, Howard helps readers to understand some of the forces that have shaped Joanne's character. Through Howard we learn that, as an idealistic political science graduate, Joanne fell in love with an ambitious young lawyer who promised her that their marriage would be one of equals, of "twin stars" who would illuminate some of the world's darkness. Howard has been part of the Kilbourns' lives from the beginning of their marriage, and he has watched while Joanne's husband, Ian, became a political star destined for great things and while Joanne became the stargazer, raising children and being a dutiful political wife. Howard's perspective on the changing nature of the Kilbourn marriage provides readers with valuable insights into many of the novels ahead.

In *A Colder Kind of Death*, Kevin Tarpley, the man who, six years earlier, brutally killed Ian Kilbourn in a seemingly senseless act on the Trans-Canada Highway, is himself murdered. Days before his death, Tarpley sends Joanne a cryptic letter implying that Ian's death was not random and that the true motive for the murder can be found in the private lives of Ian's political colleagues. As Joanne delves into the tangled relationships among Ian and the men and women whom both he and she believed were their friends, Howard—premier during that period—serves as her confidant and informant. Again his role, in addition to supporting Joanne, is to give readers the information they need to understand the plot.

Howard appears again in the seventh Joanne Kilbourn novel, *Burying Ariel*, when he attempts to heal the breach between him and his son, Charlie, by being there for him as he grieves the death of his wife. The rift between Howard and Charlie began because, as premier during Charlie's childhood and adolescence, Howard was an absentee father. Charlie's bitterness at their estrangement is at the heart of the tenth Joanne Kilbourn novel.

In *The Endless Knot*, Howard, always the rock in Joanne's life, is disintegrating. Retired, reclusive, and in his opinion redundant, the former premier is drinking heavily. When an attractive journalist convinces him to talk about his relationship with Charlie for a book she is writing about the troubled adult offspring of famous parents, Howard obliges. Charlie is livid about the book and his father's betrayal. When the journalist is murdered, Howard and Charlie are both suspects. This time it's Joanne's turn to be the rock.

In *12 Rose Street*, Howard is once again sober and solid. When Joanne discovers that Ian had an affair with her best friend that lasted from the time Joanne's first child was born to Ian's death, she is devastated. As premier of the province when Ian was attorney general, Howard was close to both Ian and Jill Oziowy, Ian's senior staff member and the woman with whom he had the ongoing affair. Howard tells Joanne that Ian believed she was stronger and more gifted than he was and that he needed to have a woman who worshipped him in his life. Howard also convinces Joanne that she must forgive Jill or be burdened with anger for the rest of her life. Once again, as a character, Howard plays a role in the development of the plot and illuminates a facet of Joanne's history and character that adds to our understanding of the experiences that have shaped my protagonist.

One final note: Howard Dowhanuik is not finished yet. I have big plans for him in the nineteenth Joanne Kilbourn novel.

The secondary characters Sally Love, Nina Love, and Desmond Love all appear on the first page of *Murder at the Mendel*, my second novel. Each character casts a long shadow over Joanne's life in the sixteen plus novels to follow.

Murder at the Mendel opens with fifteen-year-old Joanne walking in on a macabre scene at the family cottage of her best friend, Sally. Only seconds before Joanne appears, Izaak Levin, a leading New York art critic staying with the Loves, has discovered Sally's parents, still in their places at the dining table but *in extremis*. Desmond is dead; Nina's breath is a rattle, and thirteen-year-old Sally is lying on the floor. She has vomited; she is pale, and her breathing is laboured.

Joanne runs next door to get her father, a physician and Desmond's best friend from boyhood. Devastated but professional, Douglas Ellard tells Joanne and Izaak that Desmond is dead but that Nina and Sally are clinging to life.

The obvious explanation for the tragedy is heartbreaking. At the beginning of summer, Desmond, a brilliant visual artist, suffered a stroke that paralyzed the right side of his body, stilling the hand with which he made art. Unable to face a life he saw as unsupportable and leave behind his wife and the daughter he adored, he put a deadly substance in the martinis prepared for Nina and him and in the soft drink Sally always enjoyed before dinner with her parents.

After that prologue, *Murder at the Mendel* picks up thirty-two years later, on the night of the winter solstice. Joanne Kilbourn, now a professor of political science and widowed mother of three, is walking to the Mendel Gallery for the opening of a celebration of the art of Sally Love. Sally, an artist as infamous as she is famous, will be at the opening, as will her mother, Nina. The complex and tangled relationships—past and present—of the three women drive the rest of the novel and determine the direction of Joanne's life.

The Sally Love opening at the Mendel is one of the first scenes in the Shaftesbury Films made-for-TV movie *Love and Murder*, starring, among others, Claire Bloom. The Mendel Gallery of the book's title is in Saskatoon, and the marketing department at Shaftesbury decided the title should be changed to make the movie more accessible to international audiences. (Fine with me. I receive a small but tidy yearly sum from the enlightened countries that send royalties to the primary writer of a work that has been adapted for film.)

But I digress. Back to the Loves. Shaftesbury hired a visual artist to create all of the Sally Love paintings that appear in the film. We have one of them in our sunroom. The painting is large, two metres by one metre, and it's a portrait of Sally, Nina, Izaak, and Joanne in an informal gathering at the beach. The CEO of Shaftesbury chose the painting sent to me. It isn't the selection I would have made, but over the years I have come to value it because the artist obviously understood the women and positioned them perfectly to suggest their temperaments and the tensions among them. The gorgeous, bikini-wearing Sally stands confidently at the centre of the canvas; Izaak, thirty years her senior, is clearly smitten with her; Nina, a beautiful narcissist who loathes her daughter, stands with her back to Sally and Izaak, and her face is studiously impassive; Joanne, in a modest, two-piece bathing suit, stands some distance from the other figures, her hand self-consciously attempting to cover her bare midriff as she watches Sally and Izaak. Joanne's positioning on the canvas is significant. Her head is turned away from us, and we get only a glimpse of her profile.

Throughout the novels, Joanne is primarily an observer who reveals only glimpses of herself. As a first-person narrator, she is our eyes and ears, and we are privy to her reactions to the people and the events that take place in her world. I've been writing Joanne for thirty years. The average length of the novels is about 310 pages, and there are eighteen of them, so I've had 5,580 pages in which to discover my protagonist.

I still think I don't really know her. As a character, Joanne is elusive. Warm and welcoming as she is, she always seems to be withholding a part of herself, and I think this is why, as a writer, I keep coming back to her. In every novel, Joanne reveals a facet of herself that surprises me, and I always sense there is more to discover.

I have tried, unsuccessfully, to track down the original source of the following paraphrase. In a successful mystery series, the plot of each novel must be fully resolved, but the inner longings that drive the protagonist must remain unfulfilled. The protagonist's continued search for what matters most to her or him will continue to engage readers eager to see if the protagonist's dream will be realized. I think the message is clear: as a writer, you must keep alive the fire that drives your protagonist.

In *Murder at the Mendel*, Joanne tells Mieka, her nineteen-year-old daughter, that the day Desmond Love died was the day everything "went wrong." The collateral damage from his death affects Joanne for the rest of her life. The Loves are the closest thing to a family she has. Rejected by her mother, Joanne was in boarding school from the time she was six. She was one of the children teachers describe as "orphans with families"—children whose wealthy parents pay other people to raise their offspring because they don't want them around.

Her only family life comes when Joanne spends summers at the cottage with her grandmother Ellard and her father joins them for the month of August. During those summers, the Loves become her family. Sally is her best friend, Desmond is invariably kind, and Nina is the closest Joanne ever comes to having a mother.

Thirty-two years elapse before the truth emerges about what actually occurred at the Loves' cottage on the September day that opens *Murder at the Mendel*. When Joanne learns that it was Nina, unwilling to be forever burdened by an invalid husband and a daughter she loathed, who poisoned her family, it's too late. Sally has died believing that the father she loved attempted to kill her, and both Sally and Joanne have been scarred by the estrangement that began when Nina sent Sally to New York to live with Izaak immediately after Desmond's death.

Nina ostensibly offers Joanne sanctuary and unconditional love throughout her formative years. By the time Joanne learns that Nina is a coldly manipulative narcissist who has destroyed the letters Sally and Joanne sent to each other during the years after Desmond's death, the damage has been done. Joanne has suffered another painful rejection, and Sally has become a woman who sees relationships as trade-offs. She tells Joanne that becoming Izaak's lover when she was thirteen was a fair exchange: "I painted and we went to galleries and we fucked, and that was my school of the arts. . . . Not a bad preparation when you get right down to it, I guess." The loose ends of the plot of *Murder at the Mendel* are neatly tied, but the thumbprints left on Joanne's heart by those summers at the lake linger.

Four decades later, when Joanne and Zack Shreve decide to marry, he gives her a bracelet with charms representing what he terms "the whole shebang" they will own jointly after their marriage. One of the charms represents a cottage on Lawyers' Bay, a place not unlike Macleod Lake, the lake where, for one month each year, Joanne Ellard experienced what it was like to be a member of a family. From her first moment at Lawyers' Bay, Joanne is happiest and most herself when her children and later her grandchildren join Zack and her at the lake.

This is not an autobiography, but like Joanne I come from a family with complex personal dynamics. My family, too, had a cottage. I loved the freedom of summers there, and I treasured being part of the lives of the families living in the other nine cottages along our shore. After her marriage to Zack, Joanne shares her idyllic summers with the families of Zack's four law partners, friends since university. The need to recreate in adult life a happiness that in childhood was limited to summers comes from a place I know only too well.

Long ago, when I began writing *Murder at the Mendel*, my plan was to have Sally Love die at the opening of the celebration of her work. But, no matter how hard I tried, I couldn't make her death at the beginning of the novel work. As soon as she died, the light went out of the book. Finally I gave in to the inevitable, and with my godlike authorial powers I let her live—at least until close to the novel's conclusion. However, in the end, Sally won out. As a character, she was too intriguing to let go. Plot exigencies in *Murder at the Mendel* might have dictated that she be murdered, but she lives on in the expressive line of her daughter's lips and in the talent Taylor Love Shreve inherited from her. Closer to the bone, Sally lives on in Joanne's need to hold on to her.

When, after Sally's death, there is no one to take Taylor, Joanne adopts the little girl. Joanne is a pragmatist, but her decision to adopt Taylor, a child she barely knows, is not pragmatic. As she herself says in *A Darkness of the Heart*,

> There were many reasons why taking on another child, especially a child who'd been through what Taylor had been through, could have made me back away. All three of my children were still at home and I was trying to finish my dissertation so I could get tenure. Money was tight. But I never hesitated because I knew Taylor belonged with me. What I felt for her was almost primal.

Taylor is a badly damaged four year old when Joanne adopts her. The psychiatrist with whom they work says Taylor has suffered an appalling and crushing series of traumas and recommends counselling, reassurance, routine, and constant reinforcement that her new family isn't going anywhere without her.

The process is slow, and for every step forward Joanne and Taylor take there are often two steps backward. Ultimately Taylor begins to trust and to heal, but for good or ill Sally is a constant in her life. When she is very young, Taylor feels her mother's absence so acutely that Joanne often finds her tracing the lines in Sally's paintings with her small fingers because knowing that her mother touched the canvas she herself is touching makes Taylor feel happy.

Later, as an adolescent discovering herself as an artist and a young woman, Taylor reads everything she can discover about Sally online. Much of the material is salacious, and Taylor hates her mother for her promiscuity and her willingness to cast aside everything, including Taylor herself, that interfered with her art. Taylor removes all of the art her mother made from the walls of the Shreve home and turns the paintings so that only the backs of the canvases are visible.

Joanne is troubled by her daughter's anger, and when she sees two paintings Taylor has created for a charity auction she realizes how deeply rooted and twisted her daughter's feelings for Sally are.

The first painting to cause Joanne concern is titled *Blue Boy 21*. It is a large piece with the same dimensions as those of Gainsborough's famous *Blue Boy*. Taylor has kept the nature of the painting secret. She, Zack, and Joanne are in their car on their way to the art auction when Taylor reveals that she called the painting *Blue Boy*

21 because the boy in the painting is sad, not because he's wearing anything blue. In fact, she says, the boy is wearing nothing at all, and he is standing in front of a mirror.

Taylor's model for the painting has been an art student named Julian Zentner, and when Zack meets her announcement with the wry comment "So, we get full frontal Julian," Taylor's words begin tumbling over one another. "It wasn't an easy painting," she says in *The Gifted*. "A boy's body has so many different shades. I always thought a bum was a bum was a bum, but a boy's buttocks are hard to paint, and of course, their genitals are almost impossible–all those folds and different shadings." The Shreves are clearly taken aback, but Zack is game. "Well, I'm looking forward to seeing how you dealt with it," he says. Joanne, however, is troubled about what *Blue Boy 21* suggests about Taylor's relationship with her mother.

Sally Love's paintings were often overtly sexual, and the show celebrating her work at the opening of *Murder at the Mendel* showcased a particularly notorious piece. *Erotobiography* is a fresco memorializing the sexual parts of all the people with whom Sally had been intimate. Joanne notes that, according to press accounts, there were 100 individual entries, and a handful of the genitalia were female. A fresco is painted directly on the wall and becomes a permanent part of the institution that houses it. Not surprisingly, many Saskatoon citizens were uneasy about the prospect of having images of the genitalia of 100 of Sally's sexual partners preserved forever on a wall of the publicly owned Mendel Gallery.

In *The Gifted*, Joanne mentions that she has talked with Taylor about the fact that, as Sally's daughter, her work will always be closely scrutinized and compared with her mother's. Taylor knows that the art world will take note of *Blue Boy 21*. Her decision to stake her claim in Sally's territory raises questions for which Joanne has no answers.

Taylor's attitude to her own sexuality, by Joanne's account, is an uneasy one. Taylor has rebuffed Joanne's repeated efforts to approach the subject of sex by saying "All you need to know is that I'm not going to become 'a skank like my mother.' The idea of boys touching me is disgusting, and I don't ever want to talk about this again."

Seemingly Taylor has slammed the door on further discussion of her private life, but by offering *Blue Boy 21* for sale at a public charity auction she all but guarantees that a wide audience of people knowledgeable about art will see her painting. Joanne is certain that by raising her profile Taylor will open the door to questions about how she views her birth mother's promiscuity, and she fears that Taylor might use those questions as a conduit through which she can channel her anger and resentment at Sally.

Joanne's unease is underscored by the second of the works Taylor offers for public auction. *Two Painters* shows Sally and Taylor in an artist's studio. Both are working on paintings, but they have turned their backs to each other. Each woman is wholly absorbed in her own work, seemingly oblivious of the presence of the other. A large space separates the two painters.

Remembering that Taylor once remarked that painting allows her to show what she cannot say, Joanne is disturbed by the space Taylor has left between Sally and herself. It seems to be a psychological no-man's land, a space that neither painter can cross for fear of being attacked by the enemy.

At Joanne's urging, Zack makes certain his is the winning bid for *Two Painters*. Joanne has experienced her own pain at feeling deserted by Sally, and she spends hours with Taylor going through old home movies of the Love family at the lake. For the first time, Taylor sees the similarities between her mother's passion for life and art and her own. When Joanne tells her that Nina cut Sally out of her life after Desmond's death by handing her over to Izaak Levin, a man who, despite Sally's age, was certain to want a sexual relationship with her, Taylor understands that Sally did the best she could with the life she was given.

After Taylor shows Joanne that she has added a vivid Desmond Love–like abstract to the space between herself and Sally to suggest that the two painters are connected by blood, Joanne knows Taylor has found a place for her mother in her world.

Nina's place in Joanne's world is not so easily resolved. When Taylor is eighteen, Joanne shows her the portrait Sally painted of Nina, a portrait Joanne has kept hidden away, and she explains the significance Sally said the painting had for her. "When your mother gave me this, she said 'If you ever decide to take up painting, paint over any of my other pieces, but don't paint over this. It's the only painting I ever made of Nina. She was so beautiful, it almost made it possible for me to forgive her.'"

For a few minutes, Taylor is silent, leaning close to the painting to better study Nina's face. "'Her beauty is almost classically perfect,' Taylor says finally. 'Look at the degree of symmetry between the left and right half of her face. I hardly remember her, you know. But you remember her, don't you, Jo?'"

The ambivalence in Joanne's response is telling. "Nina was the centre of my world. I loved her and she loved me. Sally told me that the one good thing Nina did in her life was loving me. I've tried to hold onto that."

Taylor asks Joanne if Nina's love makes it possible for her to forget what Nina did to Sally and Desmond, and Joanne is quick to say that what Nina did was inhuman—an atrocity. Then she adds, "But I have spent years trying to sort out the evil she did to them from the good she did for me. If Nina hadn't given me a place in her world, I would have been lost. She was a monster, but she saved me."

In *A Darkness of the Heart*, Joanne learns that Desmond was her biological father. That two-and-a-half-page scene at the opening of *Murder at the Mendel* gave me characters and plot lines that became an essential part of the fabric of the next seventeen novels. At the time I wrote that scene, I had no idea whether the seeds I was planting would sprout, grow, and flourish or simply remain dormant. The one thing I did right was to give each of those characters a back story with material that might prove handy in future books. That might be information worth considering when you begin your own mystery.

STRATEGY 2

Remember Alistair MacLeod's words: "Writers write about what worries them." If you want to create a series that has a lengthy and robust life, I also recommend that you take heed of his words. Broaden your focus. Take the time to look around you. Do you see anything that worries you? Storytelling is about human connection. Is there a story you can tell that will connect your readers to behaviours, injustices, or inequities that trouble you?

Like me, my protagonist, Joanne Kilbourn, moves from Toronto to Saskatchewan. I arrived here a little earlier than Joanne, but the changes I have seen in our province are the same as the changes Joanne has witnessed. No matter where you live, the past decades will have brought radical changes in the world around you. Ask yourself the old political question: is your community a better place to live in today than it was ten, twenty, thirty, forty, or fifty years ago? Have the changes benefited everyone in your community? Who has prospered? Who has been left behind? Answering these questions might point you toward issues that will bring a new dimension to your writing and fresh life to your mystery series.

Here's my story.

Ted and I moved to Saskatchewan in 1968. The economy wasn't good. I'll never forget the number of "For Sale" signs on houses in Saskatoon. Nor will I forget the sight of farmyards dotted by shiny bins filled with wheat in danger of rotting because there were no markets and because the federal government showed no interest in addressing the crisis by helping farmers find markets. We lived in rural Saskatchewan. I had never been political, but as I watched one too many windswept small towns die before my eyes I signed up to work in our provincial election. I have been political ever since, and I have brought what I have learned about issues and electoral politics into Joanne's life.

In 1968, Saskatchewan was a have-not province. The people—proud, determined, and strong—never stopped believing that things would get better, that Saskatchewan was next-year country, and that prosperity was just around the corner.

Prosperity took its time, but it's here now with a vengeance. The wooden grain elevators are mostly gone. Saskatchewan is no longer a province dependent largely on the success of the wheat crop. Farms have become larger. Our economy is diversified. Rural residents have moved into cities. Many small towns have simply died. Our cities are booming. New housing developments are springing up like mushrooms after a three-day rain. In my neighbourhood, $300,000 family houses are purchased as tear-downs and replaced with mansions. Hi-end restaurants and trendy boutiques are flourishing. But for some of our citizens, the change has not been benevolent.

There is a great deal to worry me about the lives of those not sharing in our province's prosperity. There's a great deal to worry me in the untrammelled sprawl of our cities and in the increasing gap between the haves and the have-nots in our society. There's a great deal to worry me about the systemic racism and poverty that Indigenous peoples in Saskatchewan deal with every day. These are troubling times, but as writers we have our weapons. They're called the elements of fiction, and we can use these elements to infuse our novels with our concerns about the world around us.

Yet, a word of caution: remember always that, no matter how strongly you feel about an issue, your first obligation as a writer is to offer a powerful human story. Allow your inherently powerful material to speak for itself. Give your concerns a human face and a human heart, and you will connect with your readers, enlarge their minds, and perhaps even move them to action.

I'm going to offer an example of how I have used my writing to try to confront the racism I see happening to people around me.

My adult working life has been spent largely among Indigenous peoples. I have taught on reserves throughout Saskatchewan, and for three decades I taught at First Nations University of Canada (formerly the Saskatchewan Indian Federated College). During that time, most of my students and many of my colleagues and friends were Indigenous. The strands of those relationships are inextricably woven into the fabric of my life. My writing would not be complete if characters that reflect the people I have known were not part of it.

Because of my history, I am particularly sensitive to the issue of cultural appropriation, but when I began my series I was also aware that too often popular culture portrays Indigenous peoples as victims, criminals, or radicals demanding rights or funding. To counter these racist representations, I have tried to show in my novels the faces of Indigenous peoples as I know them to be: hardworking, proud of their kids, trying to pay off mortgages, bringing great food to communal potlucks, seeking what everyone has a right to seek—the chance to live a good life.

For example, Zack Shreve's executive assistant, Norine Macdonald, is the star athlete of Beardy's First Nation when she takes a summer job at his law firm. Intelligent, cool, and unflappable, Norine soon becomes an essential part of Falconer Shreve Altieri Wainberg and Hynd. Twenty-five years later, her salary is equivalent to that of a partner; she owns a home in the city but maintains a close relationship with Beardy's First Nation; her wardrobe is Max Mara; her accessories are handmade by Indigenous artisans.

And, though it's true that the character I created in Angela Greyeyes does play a critical role in reflecting Joanne's growing awareness that, despite repeated failures to mitigate the collateral damage caused by systemic racism and poverty, as members of a just and decent society we must never stop trying, Angela is a compelling character in her own right. She appears first on page 2 of *12 Rose Street*, and she continues to play a role in the novels that follow. At the outset, she seems doomed to a life of poverty, violence, and hopelessness, but by the sixteenth novel in the series, *What's Left Behind*, we learn that she is taking upgrading classes at the Racette-Hunter Centre, and by the eighteenth novel, *A Darkness of the Heart*, we learn that Angela, with help and hard work, has made it to being the manager of April's Place, a café/child-care centre in her North Central neighbourhood.

At the beginning of this chapter, I quoted Christopher Booker's observation in *Why We Tell Stories*: "However many characters may appear in a story, its real concern is with just one: its hero or heroine. It is he with whose fate we identify, as we see him gradually developing towards that state of self-realization which marks the end of the story." I'm not certain I wholly agree with Booker's assessment. These other characters can be more than that: they can help you to write about what concerns you, they can enable you to add substance and depth to your novels, and thus they offer a way to give your series a lengthy and robust life by writing about critical issues that matter greatly to all of us.

CHAPTER 11

EDITING

Ever tried? Ever failed? No matter.
Try again. Fail again. Fail better.
–Samuel Beckett

During one of my stints as a writer-in-residence, a friend who had also been a WIR told me about an experience she'd had. The protocol for most WIRs is the same. We ask writers to submit a fifteen–twenty-page sample of their writing and then make an appointment with them to discuss the piece. We take our commitment seriously, and as we read the submissions we write comments on the passages that work well and make suggestions about how less successful passages might be strengthened. At the appointment, the WIR and the writer talk about the best ways to develop the manuscript. It's a good system, but my friend had an emerging writer who did not take to it kindly. As soon as she spotted the comments on her manuscript, she snatched the submission off the WIR's desk. "I'm a writer, not a rewriter," she huffed, and she stomped out without giving my friend time to explain that all writers are rewriters and that the best writing any of us will ever do comes out of rewriting.

Every piece of writing is a work in progress. Over the years, I've had nine fiction editors and four dramaturges. Each has improved my work immeasurably, and each has left me with lessons that I carry with me still.

Everyone reading this book will be dealing with a very different publishing world than the one I dealt with in 1988. The manuscript of *Deadly Appearances* that I sent to Rob Sanders at Douglas and McIntyre was a mess, but Rob saw something worthwhile in it. He didn't send me the rejection letter I deserved; instead, he got me an editor—a brilliant one at that.

We've all heard the old joke: "How do you make an elephant out of a chunk of marble? Chip away everything that isn't elephant." My editor, Jennifer Glossop, chipped away everything that wasn't the novel I wanted to write, and as I said in Chapter 1 *Deadly Appearances* was nominated for what was then the W. H. Smith prize for the Best First Novel in Canada. I will be forever grateful to Rob Sanders and Jennifer Glossop for taking a chance on my chunk of marble.

These days most publishers lack the resources to pay someone to chip away at a writer's chunk of marble unless their acquisition people are certain there *is* an elephant in there. That means writers themselves have to do some serious chipping, giving their first draft a rigorous edit before sending it off.

THE EDITING PROCESS

Before you begin to edit your manuscript, take time off—two weeks minimum. You need to come at your draft with fresh eyes. There's always a period of at least six weeks before I get my first draft back from my substantive editor. I need those six weeks. The substantive editor is the one who makes the big suggestions about everything: major characters, supporting characters, plot, structure, pace, style, and whatever else simply isn't working.

My first response when I read my editor's notes on the manuscript is surly resentment. Every writer I know suffers from the "What the hell does that editor know anyway?" syndrome. The only cure for the syndrome is time and reflection.

When I've stopped wailing and gnashing my teeth, and I'm able to take a sober second look at the manuscript, I realize the value my editor's fresh pair of eyes has brought to my work. As I read her notes, there are many palm-slapping-forehead moments. I've been a writer for thirty years and a professor of English for longer than that. I'm overwhelmed and chagrined at the number of rookie mistakes I've made. "Why didn't I see that?" "Why didn't I feel how the plot lagged in the middle of the book?" "Why didn't I combine those two characters into one?" "Why didn't I clarify the killer's motivation?"" The answers to those questions are the same. I was too close to the trees to see the forest.

The first step in editing is to give yourself the distance that will allow you to approach your work as a reader would. For me that means reading the novel in hardcopy in as close to one sitting as I can manage. And it means reading without red pencil in hand. After you've read your manuscript from the reader's perspective, you're ready for the second stage.

This stage involves asking questions of your work like those listed above. In finding answers to those questions, you will be doing the work of the substantive editor. Come up with solutions and incorporate them into your second draft, and the likelihood of your work being published will be measurably better.

Now it's time for the nitty-gritty. The substantive editor will do some of this on his or her next pass through the manuscript, but I'll pass along some tips by the experts, so you can sharpen your red pencil. There's a fair amount of overlap in the rules for writing, so I'm going to extract the gist of the general rule and add a comment of my own.

WRITING TIPS

1. "Vigorous writing is concise" (William Strunk Jr.). Strunk and White's *The Elements of Style* will always be a writer's best friend. Be concise; be concrete. Cut until you can cut no more. Almost every piece of writing can be improved if you cut it by a third.
2. "Try to leave out the parts people skip" (Elmore Leonard). Deep-six your prologue. The material there is generally back story and can be worked in later. Your first task is to bring your reader into the world of your novel; start the action and write an opening that will keep your reader reading.
3. "Using Adverbs is a mortal sin" (Elmore Leonard). British writer Esther Freud's editing advice is even more draconian. Freud instructs writers to cut out

all metaphors and similes. I'm with Leonard on adverbs, but when it comes to metaphors and similes I've been known to indulge myself. I always feel terrible the next morning, but nobody's perfect.

4. "Substitute 'damn' every time you're inclined to write 'very.' Your editor will delete it and the writing will be just as it should be" (Mark Twain). Amen!
5. Don't explain too much. Give your readers credit. Allow them to become part of the creative process. In talking about Richard Price's *Lush Life*, I mentioned that Price presents his inherently powerful material without comment. If you've done your work as a writer, then your readers will do the rest.
6. Read aloud passages in your novel you suspect might be problematic. If there is a problem, then reading the passage aloud will reveal it.
7. January 24th is the feast day of Francis de Sales, the patron saint of writers and journalists. I understand he's available 24/7.
8. Enjoy the ride. Ann Patchett says, "Writing is a job, a talent, but it's also the place to go in your head. It is the imaginary friend you drink your tea with in the afternoon." Most people have to say goodbye to their imaginary friends when they start kindergarten; writers get to keep their imaginary friends forever.
9. Ray Bradbury says the most important items in a writer's make-up are zest and gusto. I agree. If you can't imagine your life without writing, then you're a real writer. Stay the course.

CHAPTER 12

GETTING PUBLISHED

This is where I wish I had a magic wand. Sadly, I don't. As I said earlier, the publishing landscape is not as welcoming to new writers as it was in 1988 when I started out. There will be times when you'll feel you've wandered into the world of *Catch-22*. You're told that publishers won't accept unagented manuscripts and that agents won't accept manuscripts from unpublished writers.

Your desk will be piled high with form letters rejecting your work. Incidentally a friend once told me she learned how to make origami toads out of rejection letters. She breathed into the toad to inflate it, gave it the name of the rejecting editor, and then stomped on it. Apparently origami toads make an immensely satisfying squishing sound when they breathe their last.

Enough of that. Onward! And that means going back to the place where we started and revisiting the two questions I posed then: "What do I hope to achieve with this piece of writing?" and "How can I best use the tools at hand to achieve my goal?"

The answer to the first question might seem simple. You now have a finished manuscript. You've done everything you can to make it publishable. What's the next step?

I suggest you go to *www.writersunion.ca/content/getting-published.* The union's advice on finding a publisher, multiple submissions, literary agents, contracts, and copyrights is direct. Its answers to questions frequently asked by emerging writers are honest but respectful. The union is realistic about the publishing landscape in Canada today but offers a path for emerging writers that gives you your best chance of being published.

When you go to the union's website, you'll notice a number of reasonably priced publications you should have. I suggest starting with the "Writers' Guide to Canadian Publishers" and the "Literary Agents" list of the thirty literary agencies in Canada with addresses and information about whether the agency is accepting new clients and what genres it accepts.

Go through the "Writers' Guide to Canadian Publishers" and make a list of the publishers that best match what you have to offer. Be realistic. Cross off the names of publishing houses unlikely to take a chance on a debut novel by an unknown writer. The firms still on your list will be your best options. Think of comparable books that have been published, and put check marks beside their publishers. My guess is that those check marks will be beside the names of some smaller publishing houses. Don't turn up your nose at them.

Go to the website of each of these publishers; carefully read the submission guidelines, and then send *exactly* what they ask for, paying particular attention to the title and spelling of the name of the editor to whom your query letter should be addressed.

Make sure your query letter has a dynamite opening sentence and paragraph. The editor reading your letter will have read thousands of query letters, but her job is to find something that will sell. Entice her. Sell your manuscript. Identify the demographic of the audience who will be lining up to buy your book. Point out what there is about you that will interest the media. Keep your letter brief. Be courteous in thanking her for giving your letter and submission serious consideration, and then write a letter to another publisher. When you've contacted all of your leads, take a break. Then start your next book.

Don't give in, and don't give up. When your floor is littered with expired origami toads, sweep them up, give them honourable burials, send out more letters, and then get back to your laptop. There's a quotation from Ursula Le Guin that you might want to print out and tape somewhere near your workspace. "The unread story is not a story," she said. "It is little black marks on wood pulp. The reader, reading it, makes it live: a live thing, a story."

Persist. Find your reader. Tell your story.

ACKNOWLEDGEMENTS

My thanks to

Howard Engel, Alison Gordon, Eric Wright, and L. R. Wright, who built a solid foundation for Canadian mystery writing.

Bruce Walsh and the University of Regina Press team for creating this series and for making the concept a reality.

My family, including Esme, who make everything possible.

SELECTED REFERENCES

Writers / Books Quoted or Discussed

Aesop, "The Lion and the Fox."
Jane Austen, *Pride and Prejudice.*
Julian Barnes, "Flaubert's Parrot," *The Sense of an Ending.*
Samel Beckett, *Worstward Ho.*
Gail Bowen, *The Brutal Heart, Burying Ariel, A Colder Kind of Death, Deadly Appearances, The Endless Knot, Kaleidoscope, The Last Good Day, Love You to Death, Murder at the Mendel (Love and Murder), 12 Rose Street, The Wandering Soul Murders, What's Left Behind, The Winners' Circle.*
Gail Bowen and Ron Marken, *1919: The Love Letters of George and Adelaide.*
Gail Bowen, Ron Marken, et al., *An Easterner's Guide to Western Canada/A Westerner's Guide to Eastern Canada.*
Beth Brant, *Food & Spirits.*
James Lee Burke, *Creole Belle.*
Raymond Chandler, "Red Wind."
Robertson Davies, *Fifth Business.*
Arthur Conan Doyle, *The Adventure of the Creeping Man, A Study in Scarlet.*
Louise Erdrich, *The Plague of Doves.*
Gillian Flynn, *Gone Girl.*
Elizabeth George, Inspector Thomas Lynley series.
Mark Haddon, *The Curious Incident of the Dog in the Night-Time.*
Joseph Hansen, Dave Brandstetter mysteries.
John Irving, *A Prayer for Owen Meany.*
Carl Gustav Jung, *Modern Man in Search of a Soul.*
Margaret Maron, Deborah Knott series.
Jay McInerney, *Bright Lights, Big City* .

Susan Neiman, *Evil in Modern Thought.*
Richard Price, *Lush Life.*
Ian Rankin, Inspector John Rebus series.
Sinclair Ross, *As for Me and My House.*
Rex Stout, *Before I Die, Murder by the Book, The Red Box, The Rubber Band, The Silent Speaker.*
Evelyn Waugh, "Work Suspended."

Interviews / reviews

James Lee Burke, interview by Anthony Rainone, *January magazine*, online, October 2004.
Michael Connelly, "Murder, Cops and the City," *International New York Times* review of Richard Price's *The Whites*, February 14, 2015.
Michael Connelly, "A Mystery with Multiple Messages," *International New York Times* review of Caleb Carr's *Surrender, New York*, August 2, 2016.
E. L. Doctorow, interview by George Plimpton, published in *The Paris Review* 101 (Winter 1986).
Vinnie Mancuso, "Ten Seconds of Black: Revisiting the Life-Affirming Series Finale of *The Sopranos*."
E. A. Robinson, interview by Joyce Kilmer, *New York Times*, April 9, 1916.
Terry Teachout, "TT: Forty years with Nero Wolfe," *About Last Night: Terry Teachout on the arts in New York City* (blog).

Writers on writing

Margaret Atwood, "Ten rules for writing fiction," *The Guardian*, 20 February 2010.
Helen Benedict, "Research in Fiction—Necessary but Dangerous: Helen Benedict on the use and mis-use of facts," www.centerforfiction.org.
Christopher Booker, *The Seven Basic Plots: Why We Tell Stories.*
Kenneth Burke, "Literature as Equipment for Living," *The Philosophy of Literary Form: Studies in Symbolic Action.*
Joseph Hansen, "The Mystery Novel as Serious Business," *The Armchair Detective*, Summer 1984).

Ernest Hemingway, advice to Arnold Samuelson, *With Hemingway: A Year in Key West and Cuba.*

Ted Hughes, "Michael Morpurgo's rules for writers," *The Guardian*, 23 February 2010.

P. D. James, "Ten rules for writing fiction," *The Guardian*, 20 February 2010.

P. D. James, "How to Write a Mystery," *Crimezine* online.

Stephen King, *On Writing: A Memoir of the Craft.*

Ursula K. Le Guin, *Dancing at the Edge of the World: Thoughts on Words, Women, Places.*

Elmore Leonard, "Ten rules for writing fiction," *The Guardian*, 20 February 2010.

Alastair MacLeod, "The Writer's Life: Geography as Inspiration," The 17th Annual Margaret Laurence Lecture, May 23, 2003.

Hilary Mantel, "Ten Rules for Writing Fiction (part 2), *The Guardian*, 20 February 2010.

Hilary Mantel, *Write* (Guardian Books)

Stephen Minot, *Three Genres: The Writing of Poetry, Fiction, and Drama.*

Vladimir Nabokov, "The Art of Literature and Commonsense."

William Strunk, Jr., and E. B. White, *The Elements of Style.*

Other

"Sherlock Holmes Museum," wikipedia.

The Wolfe Pack: The Official Nero Wolfe Society, www.nerowolfe.org.

PHOTO: MADELEINE BOWEN-DIAZ

ABOUT THE AUTHOR

Author of the award-winning Joanne Kilbourn series and of the Charlie Dowhanuik Rapid Reads novellas for reluctant readers, Gail Bowen also writes drama for radio and stage. Six of her novels have been made into TV dramas starring Wendy Crewson as Joanne Kilbourn. In 2008, *Reader's Digest* named Bowen as Canada's Best Mystery Novelist, and in 2009 she received the Derrick Murdoch Award for her contribution to Canadian crime writing from the Crime Writers of Canada. Now retired from teaching at First Nations University of Canada, Bowen lives and writes in Regina, Saskatchewan.